Predictive Analytics

Harnessing the Power of Data for Insight

Written by Daniel Carr
Published by Cornell-David Publishing House

Index

I. Understanding Predictive Analytics
1.1 Introduction to Predictive Analytics
1.2 Importance and Benefits of Predictive Analytics
1.3 Major Techniques in Predictive Analytics
1.4 Challenges in Predictive Analytics
1.5 The Future of Predictive Analytics
1.1 The Basics of Predictive Analytics
1.1.1 How Predictive Analytics Works
1.1.2 Importance of Predictive Analytics
1.1.3 Types of Predictive Analytics
1.1.4 Challenges in Predictive Analytics
1.1.5 The Future of Predictive Analytics
1.1 Predictive Analytics: The Concept Explained
1.2 Significant Components of Predictive Analytics
1.3 Applications of Predictive Analytics
1.4 Predictive Analytics Techniques
1.5 Limitations of Predictive Analytics
1.1 Defining Predictive Analytics
1.2 Methodologies and Principles behind Predictive Analytics
1.3 The Application of Predictive Analytics
1.4 Steps in Predictive Analytics Process
1.5 Challenges in Predictive Analytics
1.6 The Future of Predictive Analytics
1.1 What is Predictive Analytics?
1.1.1 The Process of Predictive Analytics
1.1.2 Applications of Predictive Analytics
1.1.3 Benefits of Predictive Analytics
1.1.4 Challenges and Limitations
II. The Essence of Data in Predictive Analysis
Chapter 4: Revealing Future Patterns with Data
The Role of Data in Predictive Analysis

How Data Shapes Predictive Modelling
Case Scenarios: Data in Action
The Challenges of Data Management
Beyond Raw Numbers: The Human Element
Conclusion
2.1 Understanding the Core Role of Data in Predictive Analysis
The Fuel for Analytical Engines
Raw Materials for Forecasting
Crucial Component for Machine Learning
Data Preparation: A Significant Step towards Quality Predictions
Data Privacy and Ethical Implications
2.1 The Value of Data in Forecasting
2.1 Understanding the Role of Data in Predictive Analysis
2.1.1 The Raw Material: Data
2.1.2 Data Quality & Suitability
2.1.3 Data Preparation and Preprocessing
2.1.4 Data Analysis
2.1.5 The Final Product: Insights & Predictions
2.1.6 Continuous Learning & Improvement
Subsection: Predictive Power of Big Data
Defining Big Data
Big Data and its Predictive Capabilities
Implementing Big Data for Predictive Analysis
III. Methods and Models in Predictive Analytics
Subsection: Exploring Regression Analysis in Predictive Analytics
A. Understanding Regression Analysis
B. Types of Regression Analysis
C. Assumptions in Regression Analysis
D. Role of Regression Analysis in Predictive Analytics
Subsection: Regression Models and Forecasting
Understanding Regression Analysis

Types of Regression
Understanding Forecasting Methods
1. Regression Analysis in Predictive Analytics
1.1 Understanding the Basics
1.2 Linear and Logistic Regression
1.3 How Does Regression Analysis Fit into Predictive Analytics?
1.4 Benefits and Drawbacks
1.5 Conclusion
3.1 Regression Analysis: A Staple in Predictive Analytics
Overview
Types of Regression Analysis
Regression Analysis and Predictive Analytics
Limitations and Cautions
Conclusion
3.1 Regression Analysis: Predicting Continues Outcomes
Linear Regression
Logistic Regression
Polynomial Regression
3.2 Time Series Models: Projecting the Future
ARIMA
Exponential Smoothing
3.3 Machine Learning: Where Predictive Analytics Meets AI
Supervised Learning
Unsupervised Learning
IV. The Power of Predictive Analytics: An Overview
1. Understanding Predictive Analytics
2. The Essence of Predictive Analytics
3. Predictive Analytics Process
4. Techniques in Predictive Analytics
5. Benefits of Predictive Analytics
6. The Impact of Big Data on Predictive Analytics
7. Predictive Analytics and Business Intelligence

8. Challenges and Limitations of Predictive Analytics
9. The Future of Predictive Analytics
IV.1 Understanding Predictive Analytics
IV.2 Applications of Predictive Analytics
IV.3 The Process of Predictive Analytics
IV.4 Power of Predictive Analytics
IV.5 Future of Predictive Analytics
The Basics and Importance of Predictive Analytics
Key Elements in Predictive Analytics
Harnessing the Power of Predictive Analytics
IV.1 Understanding the Essence of Predictive Analytics
IV.2 Scope and Impact of Predictive Analytics
IV.3 The Evolution of Predictive Analytics
IV.4 Challenges & Future of Predictive Analytics
IV.1 Understanding Predictive Analytics
IV.1.1 The Four Stages of Predictive Analytics
IV.1.2 Tools and techniques used in Predictive Analytics
IV.1.3 Applications of Predictive Analytics
V. Role of Predictive Analytics in Various Industries
5.1 The Impact of Predictive Analytics in the Healthcare Industry
5.2 Powering Financial Services with Predictive Analytics
5.3 Predictive Analytics in Retail and E-commerce
5.4 Harnessing Predictive Analytics in Manufacturing
5.5 Predictive Analytics Driving the Future of Education Sector
A. Healthcare
B. Retail
C. Finance and Banking
D. Manufacturing
E. Telecommunications
F. Energy and Utilities
Predictive Analytics in Healthcare: A Revolutionary Approach
Enhanced Patient Care

Improved Operational Efficiency

Informed Decision-Making

Drug Development and Personalized Medicine

Mental Health Predictions

5.1 Healthcare

5.2 Retail

5.3 Finance

5.4 Manufacturing

V.1. Predictive Analytics in Healthcare Industry

V.2. Predictive Analytics in the Financial Industry

V.3. Predictive Analytics in the Retail Industry

VI. Case Studies: Successful Use of Predictive Analytics

Case Study 1: Netflix's Evolving Machine Learning

Case Study 2: American Express Identifying High-quality Customers

Case Study 3: Google's Flu Trends: Predicting Public Health

VI.A Case Study: Amazon and Predictive Analytics

VI.A.1 Data Collection and Management

VI.A.2 Product Recommendations

VI.A.3 Inventory Management

VI.A.4 Fraud Detection

VI.A.5 Enhancing User Experience

VI.A.6 Conclusion

Case Study 1: Netflix- Predictive Analytics for Personalized Recommendations

Using Predictive Analytics

The Impact

Lessons Learned

Case Study 1: Starbucks - Tailoring Customer Experience with Predictive Analytics

Understanding Customer Preferences

Implementing Predictive Models

Personalization through Predictive Analytics

The Success Story

Conclusion

Case Study 1: Coca-Cola and the Power of Predictive Analytics

The Problem

The Solution

The Implementation

The Results

The Lessons

VII. Developing a Predictive Analytics Framework

7.1 Building a Strategic Predictive Analytics Framework

7.1.1 Defining Business Objectives

7.1.2 Identifying Relevant Data Sources

7.1.3 Data Collection and Integration

7.1.4 Data Cleaning and Transformation

7.1.5 Exploratory Data Analysis

7.1.6 Model Building and Evaluation

7.1.7 Deployment and Monitoring

VII.1. Understanding the Need for a Predictive Analytics Framework

VII.2. Components of a Predictive Analytics Framework

VII.3. Defining Business Objectives

VII.4. Team Building

VII.5. Data Management and Governance

7.1 Understanding the Role of Data in Predictive Analytics Framework

7.1.1 Data Anatomy in Predictive Analytics

7.1.2 The Data Collection Process

7.1.3 Data Preparation and Preprocessing

7.1.4 Building Predictive Models

7.1.5 Model Validation and Evaluation

Section VII.1: Understanding and Defining the Business Problem in Predictive Analytics

Identify and Define the Business Problem

Articulate the Objectives
Determine the Scope of the Problem
Establish Hypotheses
Prioritize Possible Solutions
VII.I. Establishing a Solid Predictive Analytics Foundation
VIII. Future Trends in Predictive Analytics
A. Predictive Analytics and AI Revolution
1. AI-driven Predictive Models
2. Real-time Predictive Analytics
3. Explainable AI
4. Autonomous Machines and Internet of Things (IoT)
5. Privacy and Security
6. Predictive Analytics in the Cloud
"Shifting Paradigms: Predictive Analytics and Artificial Intelligence"
AI and Predictive Models
Adopting AI in Businesses
Challenges and The Way Forward
1. The Impact of Artificial Intelligence on Predictive Analytics
AI Models in Predictive Analytics
Improved Predictive Accuracy
Transformation of Industries with AI-assisted Predictive Analytics
2. Arrival of Real-time Predictive Analytics
Role of IoT in Real-time Predictive Analytics
3. Automating Predictive Analytics
Impact of Automation on Workforce
8.1 Predictive Analytics and Artificial Intelligence (AI)
8.2 Ubiquity of Predictive Analytics
8.3 The Cloud and Predictive Analytics
8.4 Time-Sensitivity and Real Time Predictions
8.5 Privacy and Security Concerns
Harnessing Machine Learning for Predictive Analytics

Supervised and Unsupervised Learning
Deep Learning Revolution
Real-Time Predictive Analytics
Transparency and Ethical Concerns
IX. Challenges and Limitations of Predictive Analytics
Subsection - Understanding the Complexity and Ethical
Implications of Predictive Analytics
Data Quality and Management
Model Accuracy
Skills Gap
Transparency and Trust
Regulatory Compliance
Ethical Implications
Resistance to Change
Subsection: Understanding the Intricacies Involved in
Predictive Analytics
IX.1 Understanding the Limits of Predictive Analytics
Obstacles to Incorporating Predictive Analytics
Data Quality:
Lack of Skilled Analysts:
Data Privacy and Security Concerns:
Implementation Costs:
Misinterpretation of Output:
Ethical Considerations:
Limitations of Quantitative Analysis:
Dynamic Nature of Markets:
Understanding the Limitations of Predictive Analytics
Techniques
X. Turning Predictive Analytics into Actionable Insights
X.I. Understanding the Basics of Actionable Insights
X.II. The Process of Creating Actionable Insights
X.III. The Value of Actionable Insights in Predictive Analytics
X.Y Understanding Actionable Insights and Their Importance

X.Y.1 Translating Predictive Analytics into Actionable Insights

X.Y.2 Challenges in Harnessing Actionable Insights

X.1 Operationalizing Predictive Analytics: How to Implement Actionable Insights

X.1.1 Define Actionable Metrics

X.1.2 Building Robust Predictive Models

X.1.3 Customize Action Plans

X.1.4 Automated Response Systems

X.1.5 Foster Communication

X.1.6 Measure Outcomes

X.1 Utilization of Predictive Analysis Outputs

X.1.1 Interpreting Predictive Analysis Outputs

X.1.2 Making Predictions Actionable

X.1.3 Connecting Insights with Decision Making

X.1.4 Visualizing Predictive Analytics

"Turning Predictive Analytics into Actionable Insights"

A. Understanding the Power of Predictive Analytics

B. Transforming Predictive Intelligence into Actionable Insights

C. Pitfalls to Avoid When Generating Actionable Insights

Copyrights and Content Disclaimers:

Financial Disclaimer

Copyright and Other Disclaimers:

I. Understanding Predictive Analytics

1.1 Introduction to Predictive Analytics

Predictive analytics is a modern technology that's gradually reshaping how businesses and organizations operate. This sophisticated approach involves using historical data, machine learning algorithms, statistical methods, and AI (Artificial Intelligence) to forecast future trends, behaviours, and events. The main goal of predictive analytics is to provide businesses with actionable future insights that enable them to solve problems, capitalize on opportunities, and make data-driven decisions.

The process of predictive analytics involves several steps, including data collection, data cleaning, statistical analysis, model development, model validation and deployment, and final prediction generation. Each step plays a critical role in providing the most accurate and valuable predictions.

1.2 Importance and Benefits of Predictive Analytics

Predictive Analytics is rapidly evolving as an essential tool in the realm of business strategy and development.

- **Risk Reduction**: Predictive analysis provides insights on potential risks, enabling businesses to set up preventive measures. For instance, in finance, predictive analytics can anticipate loan defaults, credit risk, investment outcomes, and fraud detection.
- **Optimized Marketing**: It helps in optimizing marketing campaigns by offering insights on customer

responses and purchase behaviours, enabling a personalized customer journey.

- **Improved Operations**: Predictive models can streamline operational efficiency, like predicting inventory needs and managing resources.
- **Detecting Fraud**: Predictive analytics can help identify patterns and irregularities potentially indicating fraudulent activities, thus offering a robust mechanism for early alert systems.

1.3 Major Techniques in Predictive Analytics

There are three major predictive modeling techniques:

1. **Predictive models**: This technique uses predictors to forecast outcomes. Predictors used could be multiple variables such as demographics, spending habits, and previous interactions to predict outcomes like churn rate or likelihood of repurchase.
2. **Descriptive models**: This technique groups potential customers into different categories to understand the likelihood of responding to specific offers.
3. **Decision models**: They consider the correlation between predictors and specific decisions to optimize decision-making.

1.4 Challenges in Predictive Analytics

While predictive analytics brings immense benefits, certain challenges need to be overcome for its effective implementation.

- **Quality of Data**: Poor quality of data can lead to inaccurate predictions.
- **Lack of Skilled Personnel**: This field requires experts who can develop models and interpret results.
- **Changing Environments**: Real-world environments can change quickly, sometimes making models obsolete.
- **Overfitting**: It occurs when a model targets the nuances of a specific dataset so closely that it performs poorly on new data.

1.5 The Future of Predictive Analytics

With advancing technology, predictive analytics is evolving and becoming more robust. It finds new applications in diverse industries like healthcare, finance, cybersecurity, and more. From predicting patient outcomes, detecting financial fraud to predicting cybersecurity threats, predictive analytics is promising a future driven by data and actionable insights.

In essence, predictive analytics is a powerful tool that leverages technological advancements to provide data-driven decision-making ability. Understanding its importance, benefits, techniques, and challenges is the first step towards harnessing its power.

1.1 The Basics of Predictive Analytics

Predictive analytics is a branch of advanced analytics that, as the name suggests, makes predictions about future outcomes based on historical data and numerous techniques such as statistical algorithms, data mining, and machine learning.

In other words, predictive analytics utilizes the past data to predict the future. It is a proactive method for businesses to gain a competitive edge by generating actionable insights based on what is anticipated to happen. It plays a vital role in various sectors such as health care, marketing, government policies, and financial services, where it delivers immense benefits by enabling evidence-based decision making.

1.1.1 How Predictive Analytics Works

The underlying foundation of predictive analytics is based on capturing relationships between multiple explanatory variables and the predicted variable from the past occurrences and using it to predict the future. The key steps in the process include data collection, data pre-processing, statistical analysis/modeling, validation, and final implementation. While this may seem straightforward, it requires significant expertise to harness the power of algorithms, tools, techniques, and methodologies.

1.1.2 Importance of Predictive Analytics

In today's rapidly evolving business landscape, the importance of predictive analytics cannot be overstated. It assists companies in detecting fraud, optimizing marketing strategies, improving operations, and reducing risks. Beyond that, it can identify trends and patterns that would be unnoticeable in the heaps of raw data which can be invaluable for prediction of future events and enabling businesses to react proactively to those predictions.

1.1.3 Types of Predictive Analytics

Different types of predictive analytics methods are used based on the kind of prediction required and the type of data available. These include:

1. *Descriptive Models* - These classify data into different groups based on the historical data.
2. *Predictive Models* - These utilize historical data to forecast future occurrences.
3. *Decision Models* - These predict the outcomes of different decision alternatives based on known or assumed scenarios.

1.1.4 Challenges in Predictive Analytics

Although predictive analytics can deliver incredible results, utilizing it effectively is not without challenges. Data quality, data privacy, lack of skilled personnel, and time taken for data preparation and model building are some of the hurdles that businesses often face. However, with proper planning and appropriate resources, these challenges can be mitigated.

1.1.5 The Future of Predictive Analytics

Predictive analytics is not a fad that's going to fade away. Quite the contrary. With the advancements in AI and machine learning, the accuracy and usability of predictive analytics are only going to improve in the coming years. It will continue to foster significant impacts across various industries, stimulating data-driven decision making and paving the way for more optimized and efficient outcomes.

By understanding and harnessing the potential of predictive analytics, businesses can not only survive but thrive in the future competitive landscape. It's a tool that lets you look into the future to make decisions today that will set the tone for success tomorrow. Predictive analytics indeed enables businesses to go beyond knowing 'what has happened' to provide the best assessment of 'what will happen in the future'.

1.1 Predictive Analytics: The Concept Explained

Predictive analytics—a term that's been gaining quite a good deal of traction in today's data-driven age—involves the utilization of data, statistical algorithms, and machine learning techniques to identify the likelihood of future results based on historical data. To understand the concept better, consider it as "the practice of sharing informed forecasts about the future".

As digital technology evolves, companies or organizations increasingly face an influx of Big Data. Eventually, managing and deciphering such a voluminous amount of information becomes a real challenge. This is where the application of predictive analytics comes into play.

To put simply, predictive analytics examines patterns contained within this Big Data to mitigate risks and seize opportunities. It accurately forecasts what is likely to happen next so that data-informed decisions can be made in real-time.

For instance, imagine if an e-commerce company could anticipate the likelihood of a customer returning their purchase. The company could then target that person with special offers or incentives to enhance customer satisfaction and engagement.

1.2 Significant Components of Predictive Analytics

The process of predictive analytics can be broken down into several major components.

1. **Data Collection:** It all begins with data collection which involves gathering a wide variety of data from various sources such as structured, semi-structured, or unstructured data.
2. **Data Analysis:** After data collection comes data analysis. This phase necessitates experts who can analyze and mine this data to extract meaningful patterns for use in the predictive model.
3. **Statistical Analysis:** Once data has been thoroughly analyzed, statistical algorithms are applied to the data to form a statistical model.
4. **Model Deployment:** The subsequent stage involves the deployment of the predictive model using the chosen statistical algorithms.
5. **Model Monitoring:** Lastly, model monitoring is performed. It involves tracking the performance of the predictive model and fine-tuning it based on its predictive accuracy.

1.3 Applications of Predictive Analytics

Predictive analytics has far-reaching applications in several fields. In healthcare, it can be used to predict disease patterns and aid in preventive medicine. In business, it can anticipate customer behavior, optimize marketing campaigns, and detect potential risks or frauds. In finance, predictive analytics can aid in risk management, particularly in forecasting loan or credit default probabilities.

1.4 Predictive Analytics Techniques

Seamless predictive analysis is facilitated using a wide array of techniques such as regression techniques, time series analysis, machine learning, decision tree analysis, and neural networks, among others. The main distinction between these diverse techniques is the accuracy of their forecasts and the nature of the relationships they can form.

1.5 Limitations of Predictive Analytics

Despite its powerful futuristic insights, predictive analytics is not without challenges or limitations—it cannot predict the impact of unexpected, exogenous events. Furthermore, it is only as good as the data it is based on. If the data collected is biased, incomplete, or erroneous, it will yield biased, inaccurate predictions.

Moreover, the ethical implications of predictive analytics cannot be ignored. Since it often involves the processing of personal data, issues of data privacy and security pose substantial challenges. Thus, protective measures should be reinforced to ensure that the use of predictive analytics strikes the right balance, maximizing benefits, and minimizing potential threats.

1.1 Defining Predictive Analytics

To comprehend the full range of possibilities that predictive analytics offers, it is essential to start with a clear understanding of what this concept entails. In layman's terms, predictive analytics refers to the utilization of both existing data and statistical algorithms to determine the probable future outcomes of an event or a chance of occurrence.

Simply put, predictive analytics is a future-oriented data analytics technique, enabling organizations to forecast trends, patterns, and behaviors by drawing upon the computing power and statistical methodologies.

1.2 Methodologies and Principles behind Predictive Analytics

Predictive analytics is underpinned by a variety of statistical techniques and computational methodologies, including but not limited to data mining, machine learning, neural networks, AI, and statistical modeling. These methodologies seek to identify patterns by analyzing large, historical and transactional data sets, to predict future outcomes.

A quintessential element of predictive analytics is the predictor variables which wield information about the probable behaviors. These variables are used in conjunction with a predictive model to foretell with reasonable accuracy about the future events.

1.3 The Application of Predictive Analytics

Predictive analytics finds usage in a broad spectrum of disciplines, sectors, and industry verticals. Companies have applied the power of predictive analytics in the area of marketing, finance, healthcare, insurance, and telecommunications among others.

A few of its typical applications include, credit scoring, fraud detection, market segmentation, inventory and supply-chain optimization, customer lifetime value modeling, churn prediction, health risk assessment, and predictive maintenance.

1.4 Steps in Predictive Analytics Process

The process of predictive analytics can be delineated in several comprehensive steps: data collection, data pre-processing, model development, testing and validation, and deployment. Each step entails specific procedures and methodologies.

- **Data collection:** The first and foundational phase is to collect a vast, historical dataset.
- **Data pre-processing:** After data collection, one needs to preprocess it, addressing missing values, outliers, and fitting the data in a suitable structure for analyses.
- **Model development:** Then, based on the data at hand and the problem to be addressed, a predictive model is developed.
- **Testing and Validation:** The accuracy and reliability of the model are evaluated in this step to ascertain its effectiveness.
- **Deployment:** The final step involves implementing the model onto the real data to make future predictions.

1.5 Challenges in Predictive Analytics

While predictive analytics provides powerful insights and forecasts, it is not devoid of challenges. Issues such as data privacy, data quality, the accuracy of models, and the necessity of skilled analysts may pose challenges to implementing predictive analytics.

1.6 The Future of Predictive Analytics

Going forward, predictive analytics is set to become even more sophisticated and pervasive as data continues to grow exponentially. The future of predictive analytics resides in the evolving technologies like AI, machine learning, and deep learning. Incorporating these technologies allows us to create more accurate predictive models, capable of learning and adapting to new data, thereby continually improving the accuracy of predictions.

In conclusion, getting to grips with predictive analytics, understanding its potentials, limitations, and future prospects, would enable individuals and organizations to harness the power of data for valuable, future insights.

1.1 What is Predictive Analytics?

Predictive analytics is a branch of advanced analytics that uses techniques from data mining, statistics, modeling, machine learning, and artificial intelligence (AI) to analyze current data and make predictions about future events. By examining historical and real-time data, these analytics provide insights into what may happen in the future, enabling informed decision-making.

The power of predictive analytics lies in its ability to generate actionable insights about the future. This allows businesses and organizations to anticipate risks, discover opportunities, enhance operation efficiency, improve products, and bolster strategic management by leveraging their data to not only understand what has happened but also to get a glimpse of what may come.

Predictive analytics consist of various statistical techniques and advances in machine computing that makes it possible to predict future occurrences based on historical data. This could range from predicting customer behavior to making future business forecasts.

1.1.1 The Process of Predictive Analytics

At its core, predictive analytics is about extracting information from data sets and determining patterns that can forecast future outcomes with a reasonable amount of certainty. The process can be broken down into several key steps:

- **Data Collection:** This first step involves gathering the required data. From transaction records to customer feedback, predictive analytics can handle both structured and unstructured data from multiple sources.
- **Data Cleaning:** This step entails preprocessing and cleaning the data. It's about dealing with missing or inconsistent data and ensuring the data used is of high quality.
- **Data Analysis:** The main bulk of predictive analytics lies in this stage, which involves analyzing and interpreting the data using statistical models and algorithms.
- **Model Building:** Here, data analysts use various predictive models to learn and understand the relationships among different attributes of data.
- **Validation Testing**: Before a predictive model can be deployed, it must be rigorously tested to ensure its reliability and effectiveness.
- **Deployment and Monitoring**: Once validated, the predictive model is deployed and constantly monitored to guarantee its accuracy in predicting future outcomes.

Predictive model design and implementation, however, depend on the specific use case and the kind of data available. It is a complex process that requires sophisticated software tools, skilled personnel, and proper management.

1.1.2 Applications of Predictive Analytics

Predictive analytics has a wide array of applications across multiple industries. Here are some typical uses:

- **Forecasting Trends**: Companies can use predictive analytics to predict market trends and identify growth opportunities.
- **Customer Behavior Predictions**: Businesses can predict customer behavior, anticipate churn and tailor marketing strategies effectively.
- **Inventory Management**: Predictive analytics can deliver accurate demand forecasting for optimal inventory management.
- **Risk Management**: Financial institutions can better manage risks by predicting possibilities of fraud or default.
- **Healthcare**: Predictive models can be used to predict disease outbreaks or patient readmissions.

1.1.3 Benefits of Predictive Analytics

By leveraging predictive analytics, organizations can gain a competitive advantage in today's data-driven era. The benefits are numerous:

- **Enhanced Decision Making**: By predicting future scenarios, businesses can make strategic, data-driven decisions.
- **Improved Risk Management**: Predictive analytics allows for more effective risk management by identifying potential risks before they become big issues.
- **Increased Operational Efficiency**: With the insights obtained, businesses can optimize resources, improve productivity and reduce costs.
- **Better Customer Service**: Predicting customer behavior can help businesses offer personalized services and strengthen customer relationships.

1.1.4 Challenges and Limitations

While predictive analytics offers countless benefits, it also poses its fair share of challenges:

- **Data Quality**: For accurate results, high-quality data is a must. Low-quality data can lead to inaccuracies and unreliable predictions.
- **Complexity of Models**: Building predictive models requires advanced technical skills and understanding of complex algorithms.
- **Privacy Concerns**: With the use of data comes the risk of breaching privacy regulations.

Predictive analytics isn't about having a crystal ball that guarantees the future, but it provides the best possible indicators of what to expect. Therefore, it's important to remember that while predictions may be highly accurate, they aren't a 100% certainty. Predictions should thus be used as guidance and not as absolute truth.

Predictive analytics is undoubtedly a powerful tool, but like any other tool, its effectiveness ultimately depends on how it's used. In the right hands, it can help unlock invaluable insights, drive strategic decision-making, and usher businesses into a new era of data-driven growth. However, without a robust implementation strategy and responsible data practices, the power of predictive analytics may remain unrealized.

II. The Essence of Data in Predictive Analysis

Chapter 4: Revealing Future Patterns with Data

In this chapter, we will delve deep into the inner workings of predictive analytics, and the critical role played by data in making informed predictions. The choice of the relevant datasets being used, and the efficiency of the algorithms applied, directly affects the quality of the insights and predictions generated.

The Role of Data in Predictive Analysis

Data is the raw material for predictive analytics. Just as a sculptor carefully chooses the right stone before starting their work, a data analyst must start with the right dataset to gain accurate predictions. The important point here is not the sheer quantity of data but the quality and precision of the data that fit the given problem.

Data of various formats such as unstructured, semi-structured, and structured data are used in predictive analytics. Data, once pre-processed, cleaned, and transformed, provides the foundation upon which predictive models are built.

How Data Shapes Predictive Modelling

Predictive modelling takes these data sets and applies a variety of statistical techniques to it, such as machine learning and predictive modeling, to analyze current and historical facts to make predictions about the future.

The involved mathematical models sieve through extensive datasets to spot significant patterns and trends. The predictive models evolve over time as they continue to consume newer data and revise the predictions according to the observed data changes.

Case Scenarios: Data in Action

To visualize the power of predictive analytics, consider a movie streaming service that recommends films based on users' previously watched items. Here, the data points would include the films each user has viewed and maybe even how they rated each movie. Or consider a credit card company that uses predictive analytics to detect fraudulent transactions. In this case, the company collects data points on each card user's typical purchase behavior to detect anomalies that may indicate fraud.

The Challenges of Data Management

While the advancing technology has granted us easy access to vast amounts of data, it brings with it its fair share of challenges. Handling large amounts of data requires powerful processing capacities, efficient storage solutions, and the know-how to manage and maintain all of this.

Moreover, data privacy and security have become prime concerns in the modern world. A robust mechanism is required to secure sensitive data while ensuring that privacy regulations are complied with.

Beyond Raw Numbers: The Human Element

It's crucial to remember that while data is at the heart of predictive analytics, a human touch can often deliver the most profound insights. Analysts play a critical role in interpreting the data correctly, understanding what makes relevant metrics significant, or spotting a significant trend.

Conclusion

To summarize, data is the lifeblood that fuels predictive analytics. With the exponential growth of data in this digital world, the potential of predictive analytics to revolutionize industries and transform businesses is tremendous. However, it requires carefully designed models, precise application, and a comprehensive understanding to unlock this potential.

In the following chapters, we'll delve deeper into each step of the predictive analytics process, discussing the techniques and tools used at each stage, and exploring how to interpret and apply the results effectively to drive decision-making and innovation.

2.1 Understanding the Core Role of Data in Predictive Analysis

Undeniably, data is the lifeblood of predictive analytics. The inherent power of data lies in its ability to provide insights into patterns and trends. These insights consequently enable strategic planning, decision-making, and predictions about future outcomes.

The Fuel for Analytical Engines

A predictive model is like a machine. Just like machines run on fuel, predictive models run on data. Without data, these models could not function. In this respect, data can be viewed as the fuel that drives the engine of predictive analytics.

Numerous types of data can power the predictive analytics engine, and this becomes more apparent in the era of big data. Structured data such as numerical and categorical data, unstructured data like text and images, and semi-structured data such as XML and JSON, all possess the potential to be converted into useful insights.

Raw Materials for Forecasting

Predictive analytics involves extracting information from existing data sets with the aim of predicting future probabilities and trends. In other words, data is the raw material used to create forecast products. The quality of the raw materials (data) directly influences the quality of the final product (prediction). Incomplete or inaccurate data would inevitably lead to inaccurate predictions.

Crucial Component for Machine Learning

Data not only fuels predictive analytics but also acts as a crucial component for machine learning (ML), a key technique used in predictive analytics. Machine learning models learn from data to make predictions or decisions without being explicitly programmed.

In supervised learning, labeled data is used to train the ML model, and the model learns to predict the outcome from the features of the input data. However, in unsupervised learning, the model identifies patterns and relationships in the input data. Consequently, the quality, diversity, and volume of the data significantly impact the performance of ML models.

Data Preparation: A Significant Step towards Quality Predictions

Although data is a critical resource in predictive analytics, it should be adequately cleansed and transformed before utilization. Data preparation involves formatting, cleaning, and sampling the data, which directly affects the quality of predictive analysis. Invalid or inconsistent data can lead to erroneous conclusions, while biased data can lead to discriminatory predictions. Therefore, diligent data preparation is necessary for establishing successful predictive analysis models.

Data Privacy and Ethical Implications

While data is the essence of predictive analysis, it's critical to respect data privacy and abide by ethical considerations in data handling and analytics. Predictive analytics should never violate a person's privacy rights nor should it be used unethically. Therefore, appropriate data governance mechanisms should be put in place to ensure data privacy, accuracy, accessibility, and integrity.

In conclusion, data's role is integral to predictive analytics, performing various roles across different stages, from the raw material for analyses to the learning material for ML models. However, its power is only as potent as the handling is careful—data preparation and privacy must be prioritized to derive meaningful and ethical insights. By acknowledging and leveraging these various facets of data's importance in predictive analytics, we can effectively harness its power for future insights.

2.1 The Value of Data in Forecasting

In the sphere of predictive analytics, data is the lifeblood that gives this scientific approach its predictive power. This section delves deep into the role of data, the reasons behind its significance, and how it is transformed into potent predictive insights that drive business strategy and decision-making.

a) The Role of Data in Predictive Analytics

Any discussion of predictive analytics would be incomplete without first emphasizing the fulcrum of the operation: data. In predictive analytics, data is the raw material. Every prediction, every forecast hinges upon the quality and quantity of data available. Data is the foundational building block for predictive models — models that are capable of learning from historical and real-time data, discerning patterns, and making educated predictions about future events or outcomes.

b) Quality and Quantity of Data

- *Quantity*: An increased volume of data amplifies the ability of a model to learn and make precise predictions. The vast amount of data generated every minute on social media, IoT, mobile devices, websites, and businesses across various sectors, is generally called 'Big Data'. The omnipresence of Big Data has magnified the opportunities for predictive analysis in unimaginable ways.
- *Quality*: The accuracy and importance of data equally matters. Garbage In, Garbage Out (GIGO) principle echoes this sentiment. If the input data is flawed, so will be the output. In this context, the process of data cleansing becomes critical to predictive analytics. It involves identifying and rectifying (or removing) inaccurate data from a database. The end goal is to improve data integrity and the degree of predictions.

c) Data Processing and Management

Predictive Analysis leverages data, both structured and unstructured. Structured data includes anything that can be neatly placed into tables, graphs, or charts, while unstructured data includes videos, images, text data, emails, etc. Data management involves safely and efficiently storing these varied data forms, making sure they are accessible for processing. The process includes several pivotal stages like data collection, data preprocessing, data integration, data transformation, and data reduction.

d) Deriving Predictive Insights from Data

Raw data won't confer any predictive power just by itself; it must be controlled, transformed, and processed to elicit the patterns buried within. The steps are usually along these lines:

- *Data Collection*: This is the initial stage, where relevant data is gathered from various sources.
- *Data Preprocessing*: This stage aims to clean and format the data. It may involve dealing with missing or inconsistent data, noise reduction, and data normalization.
- *Model Building*: This occurs once the data is clean and ready for use. During this stage, relevant algorithms are applied, forming the predictive model.
- *Assessment & Validation*: The model is then tested, validated, and its performance is evaluated. This can reveal any needed improvements.
- *Deployment & Monitoring*: The final predictive model is implemented in a real-world environment for actual predictions and continuously monitored for performance.

Predictive analytics demands immense care in managing, processing, and analyzing data. The data quality and quantity play a pivotal role in determining the accuracy of the model built, thereby offering more reliable future insights for better decision making. Specific tools, technologies, and strategies are used to amplify the data's value within predictive analytics, making it an instrumental force in this field.

2.1 Understanding the Role of Data in Predictive Analysis

In understanding the essence of predictive analysis, it is paramount we investigate the pivotal role data plays in its entire operations. Predictive analysis, at its core, relies heavily on data. This is because it involves using data from past events, processing and analyzing these data to form patterns that can predict future outcomes or trends. It is within this context that the importance of data in predictive analysis can be fully understood and appreciated.

2.1.1 The Raw Material: Data

Data serves as the raw material in the predictive analysis process. Like a goldsmith requires gold to create a beautiful piece of jewelry, a predictive analyst requires data to create insightful forecasts. The process of predictive analysis thus begins with the capturing, gathering, or collection of data. Data can emerge from a range of different sources - from transactional records in a business to survey results, or even from social media posts. The importance here is that without data, predictive analysis isn't possible.

2.1.2 Data Quality & Suitability

Not all data is created equal, and thus not all data is equally suitable for predictive analysis. The success of any predictive model largely depends on the quality of data fed into it. It is essential for predictive analysts to use accurate, consistent, and reliable data. Poor quality data can lead to inaccurate predictions, misleading results, or even completely erroneous conclusions.

2.1.3 Data Preparation and Preprocessing

Data seldom comes in a ready-to-use format. It often needs to be cleaned, formatted, or preprocessed before it can be used for predictive analysis. This phase involves several tasks such as handling missing values, removing outliers, data transformation, and feature scaling. The objective here is to ensure data are of the right quality, format, and structure to be used effectively in the predictive model.

2.1.4 Data Analysis

Once data is collected and prepared, the analysis phase begins. Here, algorithms and analytical tools are used to examine, interpret, and analyze data. For instance, statisticians may perform regression analysis to identify relationships among variables. Machine learning models may be used to recognize patterns in data. The goal here is to derive actionable insights from data that can be used to predict future outcomes.

2.1.5 The Final Product: Insights & Predictions

The ultimate value of data in predictive analysis is in the insights and predictions that can be derived from it. These insights could help organizations make informed strategic decisions, optimize their operations, or even open up new opportunities for growth. The predictions made from data can provide glimpses into the future, offering businesses the chance to stay ahead of the curve, anticipate customer needs, or mitigate potential risks.

2.1.6 Continuous Learning & Improvement

Data in predictive analysis is not a one-time-use resource. Even after the initial analysis, the data should be retained for further learning and improvement. This is because the real-world environment is dynamic and subject to constant change. By continuously monitoring and tracking performance, and updating models based on new data, predictive analysis can help organizations to learn, adapt, and improve on an ongoing basis.

In a nutshell, the critical role of data in predictive analytics is unquestionable. It is essentially the lifeblood that fuels the predictions. Having a clear comprehension of its role can go a long way in creating effective predictive models. It is indeed that omnipotent tool in the hand of an analyst, which if harnessed correctly, can turn business uncertainties into opportunities.

Subsection: Predictive Power of Big Data

In the realm of predictive analytics, data forms the foundation. The volume, velocity, variety, and veracity of data, collectively known as the 4Vs of Big Data, profoundly influence the results of any predictive analysis.

Defining Big Data

"Big Data" is a terminology derived to describe data so abundant and complex that traditional data processing tools encounter difficulty to manage. The essence of Big Data feeds into its predictive potential. The more data you possess, the more patently you can observe patterns, trends and associations, particularly relating to human behavior.

Big Data and its Predictive Capabilities

Capturing data in huge volumes, often in real-time, gives businesses an edge in terms of predictive analytics.

- **Volume**: The extent of data available today is inconceivable. Social media feeds, internet sensors, machine logs, digital images and videos, purchase transaction records, cellphone GPS signals, among others, render inconceivable volumes of data every second. This ample data aids complex predictive models by providing wider variables and clearer patterns.
- **Velocity**: The speed at which we receive data is equally critical. Faster data means quicker predictions, particularly vital to industries that need to react in real-time or near real-time such as finance, health and e-commerce.
- **Variety**: The diversity or range of data, from structured to semi-structured to unstructured data, fuels the richness and depth of information for predictive analysis. The broader the assortment, the better the insights.
- **Veracity**: This connotes the uncertainty of available data. Given that data can often be messy - unclean, unstructured, and containing anomalies - the ability to differentiate credible, accurate data from the noise is important.

Implementing Big Data for Predictive Analysis

The expansive scope of Big Data paves the way for more complex predictive analysis, freeing practitioners from traditional constraints. Incorporating vast, varied data enhances the predictive model enabling more precise decision-making. Integrating Big Data into predictive analytics involves:

- **Data Mining**: Extraction of relevant data points from extensive data sets is essential. Identifying patterns enables prediction of future trends.
- **Predictive Modelling**: Employing statistical techniques and algorithms to anticipate future outcomes is the core of predictive analytics. The larger and more diverse the data set, the more accurate are the model's forecasts.
- **Machine Learning**: As a subset of artificial intelligence, machine learning feeds on Big Data to make accurate predictions. When exposed to more data, these ML models continually learn and adapt, sharpening their accuracy over time.

Predictive analytics powered by Big Data proposes many inventive avenues for industry practices. With the right application of technology, organizations can turn the data flow into a strategic advantage – predicting customer's next purchase, anticipating machine failures, detecting fraudulent transactions, improving healthcare diagnosis - transforming the way industries think, work and grow.

In this era of data abundance, predictive analytics is fast becoming a game-changer. Big Data, harnessed smartly, opens up untapped potential, enabling organization to foresee what lies ahead and act proactively to seize the opportunities of tomorrow.

III. Methods and Models in Predictive Analytics

Subsection: Exploring Regression Analysis in Predictive Analytics

Regression analysis is one of the powerful statistical methods used in predictive analytics that is used to identify and analyze the relationship between a dependent variable and one or more independent variables. It is one of the many predictive modeling techniques, and it is used for forecasting, time series modeling, and determining the causal-effect relationship between variables.

A. Understanding Regression Analysis

The term "regression" refers to a regression of y upon x. That is, it means predicting the approximate y in "y = f(x)" when only the sampling of x is given. Regression analysis helps to understand how the typical value of the dependent variable or criterion variable changes when any one of the independent variables is varied, while the other independent variables are held fixed.

B. Types of Regression Analysis

There are several types of regression analysis; however, a few remain more commonly used in predictive analytics.

1. Linear Regression: It is a statistical approach to model the relationship between two variables (dependently and independently) by fitting a linear equation to observed data. It can be divided further into two types; simple linear regression and multiple linear regression.

2. Logistic Regression: Unlike linear regression which predicts continuous values, logistic regression is used to model the probability of a certain event occurring like pass/fail, win/lose, alive/dead or healthy/sick.

3. Polynomial Regression: If the power of independent variable is more than 1, the equation becomes a polynomial, hence named as polynomial regression. It fits a nonlinear relationship between the value of x and the corresponding conditional mean of y.

4. Ridge Regression: Ridge Regression serves as a solution to the multicollinearity problem by assigning a degree of bias to the regression estimates.

5. Lasso Regression: Lasso (Least Absolute Shrinkage and Selection Operator) Regression is like Ridge Regression but has the ability to reduce the variability and improve the accuracy of linear regression models.

C. Assumptions in Regression Analysis

In regression analysis, there are several assumptions made:

- *Linearity*: The relationship between predictors and the target is linear.
- *Independent errors*: The residuals/errors of the model should be independent of each other.
- *Normality*: For any fixed value of X, Y is normally distributed.
- *Equal variances*: For any fixed value of X, the variance of Y is constant.

D. Role of Regression Analysis in Predictive Analytics

In predictive analytics, regression analysis is used to predict outcomes and assess potential relationships between variables. It helps in understanding the future scenarios in various fields like market research, product profitability, real estate, weather prediction, healthcare, the stock market, etc.

Given the increasing access and availability of data, the role of regression analysis in predictive analytics is proving to be of paramount importance. It offers a simple, yet powerful means of tuning into data, and making calculated, future-focused decisions as a result.

Despite being based on a simple concept of linear relationship, its simplicity has won it great importance in the realm of business understanding. It can assist in creating a future course or pave the road for changes needed today to affect the future positively.

In conclusion, regression analysis is a critical tool in predictive analytics. It may not always deliver flawless predictions—because real-world data is messy and unpredictable—but if implemented correctly, it can yield incredibly valuable insights that drive better business decision-making. Thus, understanding its subtleties and nuances, as well as knowing when and how to use it, are must-have skills for today's data analysts and scientists.

Subsection: Regression Models and Forecasting

One of the major methods and models used in predictive analytics is the **Regression Models and Forecasting Techniques.** These methods are cherished due to their flexibility, ease of understanding, and robustness, which means they can take many forms and are very adaptable to a multitude of applications.

Understanding Regression Analysis

Regression analysis is a powerful statistical technique that allows analysts to examine the relationship between two or more variables. It embodies the simplicity of correlation and progresses to the prediction of one variable from the one or more others. The dependent variable is often denoted Y, while the independent variables are represented by the symbol X.

The significant applications of regression models in predictive analytics extend from forecasting of future sales in business, prediction of disease progression in medicine, estimating crop yields in agriculture, predicting climate change effects on ecosystems, and many more.

Types of Regression

Several types of regression models can be used in predictive analytics. Each has unique features that make it suitable for specific situations. Here are a few types:

1. **Simple Linear Regression**: One independent variable is used to predict the outcome of the dependent variable. For instance, the relationship between age and blood pressure.
2. **Multiple Linear Regression**: Used when there are two or more independent variables. If used in marketing, for example, multiple linear regression can gauge the impact of changes in the price of goods, marketing expenditures, and the impact of social media advertising on sales.
3. **Polynomial Regression**: This type extrapolates the relationship between the independent variable and the dependent variable as an nth degree polynomial.
4. **Ridge Regression**: Used to analyze multiple regression data that suffers from multicollinearity, which happens when independent variables are highly correlated.
5. **Logistic Regression**: This type is used when the dependent variable is binary. For example, whether a

patient has a disease (yes/no), or whether an email is spam (yes/no).

Understanding Forecasting Methods

Forecasting methods constitute another important tool in predictive analytics. Unlike regression, which predicts a variable value based on the actual values of other variables, **forecasting predicts future values of the same variable**. More precisely, forecasting embeds the belief that the patterns in the data that we observe now will continue into the future.

There are multiple classes of forecasting methods:

1. **Qualitative techniques**: Often used when there isn't any hard data available and relies on expert opinion and other less objective information.
2. **Time series forecasting**: Here, historical data is analyzed to extrapolate the data into the future. This includes methods like moving averages, exponential smoothing, and autoregressive models.
3. **Causal models**: These models assume that the variable being forecasted is influenced by one or more other variables. The model will forecast the variable of interest, provided that the predictor variable's future value is known.
4. **Artificial Intelligence (AI) forecasting methods**: More recently, machine learning and deep learning techniques are being applied to forecasting. Depending on the particular algorithm, these may considered a form of causal model forecasting or time series forecasting.

In conclusion, the rich variety of regression models and forecasting techniques provides analysts with a versatile toolkit to tackle the different challenges that come with predicting the future. Mastering these techniques and understanding when to apply which technique is a key skill in predictive analytics.

1. Regression Analysis in Predictive Analytics

Regression analysis can be simply defined as a powerful statistical analysis technique used to explain or predict the change in one variable (dependent variable) due to changes in other variables (independent variables). The concise nature of this technique, coupled with its high accuracy, has made it a popular choice for predictive analytics in different fields such as finance, healthcare, retail, and more.

1.1 Understanding the Basics

The easiest way to understand regression analysis is by considering a simple example. Suppose a retailer wants to determine how much the sales of a particular product fall or rise based on its price. Here, the price can be considered as an independent variable, while the sales is the dependent variable. A regression analysis will use existing data points to build a model which accurately predicts how a change in price might alter sales.

1.2 Linear and Logistic Regression

There are various types of regression models, but the two most commonly used are linear and logistic regressions.

Linear Regression: This type of regression analysis helps in predicting a continuous dependent variable based on one or more independent variables. Think about predicting a house price (dependent variable) based on variables such as location, size, and age of the house (independent variables).

Logistic Regression: This is used when the dependent variable is categorical, meaning it can take one out of limited possible values. For instance, whether a customer will churn or not (Yes/No), or predicting if an email is spam or not (Spam/Not Spam).

1.3 How Does Regression Analysis Fit into Predictive Analytics?

Predictive analytics uses historical data to predict future outcomes. The essence of this approach lies in identifying patterns or relationships between variables from past data to forecast how they might behave or correlate in the future. And this is precisely where regression analysis comes into play.

Regression analysis, by nature, is equipped to identify relationships between variables, quantify their strength, and use these correlations to build reliable predictive models. This makes it a vital tool of predictive analytics.

1.4 Benefits and Drawbacks

Benefits:

- It's relatively simple to understand and explain.
- Regression analysis can deal with multiple input features at once.
- It provides a quantified measure of the strength of the relationship between variables.

Drawbacks:

- Linear regression assumes a linear relationship between variables which might not always be true.

- It's sensitive to outliers and can lead to inaccurate predictions if the dataset contains too many of them.

1.5 Conclusion

Despite its limitations, regression analysis remains an essential tool in the predictive analytics toolbox. It is a relatively simple yet powerful technique to analyze past data and uncover patterns that can be useful for making accurate predictions in different areas such as business, healthcare, and more.

Remember, though, while regression analysis can unearth relationships and patterns, it doesn't establish a cause-effect relationship between variables. Thus, a high degree of caution should be exercised while interpreting and acting on the results of a regression analysis.

In the next subsection, we will discuss another important method in predictive analytics- Decision Trees. Stay tuned!

3.1 Regression Analysis: A Staple in Predictive Analytics

Regression Analysis is a paramount tool under the Predictive Analytics umbrella, serving as a foundation in understanding and quantifying the relationships between different variables. At its core, it seeks to predict a dependent variable based on the value(s) of at least one independent variable.

Overview

In the simplest form, regression analysis could be a linear regression model, which attempts to draw a straight line that best fits the data points available. This line represents a mathematical equation where the dependent variable (for example, sales revenue) can be estimated based on the independent variable(s) (such as advertising expenditure).

Primarily, this tool is used to understand which among independent variables are related to the dependent variable, and to explore the forms of these relationships. In more complex situations, it helps in predicting the future based on patterns formed in data.

Types of Regression Analysis

There are many types of regression analysis, each serving a different purpose and accommodating a variety of data frameworks. Here are the primary types:

- **Linear Regression:** As the simplest type, it assumes a linear relationship between the dependent and independent variables. It calculates the line of best fit using the least squares method.
- **Multiple Regression:** When you have more than one independent variables, you can use the multiple regression model to predict the dependent variable.
- **Logistic Regression:** Used specifically when the dependent variable is binary or categorical, such as 'yes' or 'no.'
- **Polynomial Regression:** Used when the power of some independent variable is more than 1. It provides a curved line to commit to the data points.

Regression Analysis and Predictive Analytics

In the realm of predictive analytics, regression analysis is invaluable. It not only enables prediction of significant variables but also provides the ability to create data-driven actionable insights.

For instance, an eCommerce business can use regression analysis to predict future sales based on data points like historical sales, website traffic, and marketing campaign effectiveness. Similarly, a healthcare institute could use it to gauge patient readmission rates based on past admission patterns, patient demographics, and treatment protocols.

Regression models can also be used to predict key operational metrics, business trends, financial forecasts, and to plan efficient resource allocation. Moreover, it augments Machine Learning systems with enhanced predictive capability.

Limitations and Cautions

However, as powerful as it is, regression analysis does carry some cautioning notes. The accuracy of the results depends on the quality of the data used – if there are biases or skewness in the data, it can lead to incorrect predictions. Correct use of regression analysis also involves checks for appropriateness, significance, and goodness of fit.

Furthermore, it is essential to note that regression analysis directly follows the saying "correlation does not imply causation." Although it can be used to identify correlations and relationships, it doesn't provide proof of a causal relationship between the independent and dependent variables.

Conclusion

Despite these caveats, the regression analysis is an integral workhorse in predictive analytics. Used thoughtfully, it can provide valuable insights into the complex interdependencies of variables, allowing organizations to predict future outcomes and make more informed decisions.

3.1 Regression Analysis: Predicting Continues Outcomes

One of the most commonly used statistical techniques in predictive analytics is regression analysis. Regression models are used to predict a continuous or categorical dependent variable based on one or more independent variables. The computational power of regression models relies on establishing the relationship between predictors (independent variables) and the outcome (dependent variable), in order to make predictions on unseen data.

Linear Regression

Linear Regression is a common type of regression analysis that quantifies the relationship between a continuous dependent variable and one (simple linear regression) or more independent variables (multivariable linear regression). The term "linear" refers to the relationship between the independent and dependent variables, which is represented by a straight line in a scatterplot. The goal is to estimate the coefficients of the mathematical equation to minimize the difference between the actual and predicted values.

Logistic Regression

Logistic regression, a type of binomial regression, is another popular method used in predictive analytics. The output is a probability that the given input point belongs to a certain class. In other words, it measures the relationship between a categorical dependent variable and one or more independent variables by estimating probabilities using a logistic function. One major advantage of logistic regression is that it provides probabilities and is adaptable to multiclass classification.

Polynomial Regression

Polynomial regression is a form of regression analysis in which the relationship between the independent variable and the dependent variable is modeled as an nth degree polynomial. This can model relationships between variables that aren't linear and can bend with the data.

A good predictive analytics model needs to not only fit the historic data well, but should also accurately predict future events. Adequate regression analysis should end not just with creating the model, but also testing and validating it to ensure a robust and reliable prediction.

3.2 Time Series Models: Projecting the Future

Time series analysis involves developing models that predict future values based on previously observed values. The methods are primarily employed in financial and economic forecasting, but also in engineering, geophysics, and neuroscience. Some of the popular time series analysis methods include the AutoRegressive Integrated Moving Average (ARIMA) and Exponential Smoothing.

ARIMA

ARIMA, short for 'AutoRegressive Integrated Moving Average', is actually a class of models that 'explains' a given time series based on its own past values, that is, its own lags, the lagged forecast errors, and the trend of the time series. It is an extension of the simpler AutoRegressive Moving Average and adds the notion of integration.

Exponential Smoothing

Exponential smoothing methods are time series forecasting methods for univariate data that use an exponentially decreasing weight for past observations. This method involves calculating the moving average where the weights decrease exponentially. This gives more importance to recent observations while still not discarding older observations completely.

3.3 Machine Learning: Where Predictive Analytics Meets AI

Machine learning is the backbone of predictive analytics, helping to understand patterns in vast datasets and predict future data behavior. In the context of predictive analytics, machine learning algorithms are categorized as supervised and unsupervised learning.

Supervised Learning

In supervised learning, an algorithm learns from labeled training data, and makes predictions based on that data. A typical supervised learning task is classification, where the algorithm categorizes data into a predefined set of classes. Another task is regression, aiming to predict a numerical outcome.

Unsupervised Learning

Unsupervised learning, on the other hand, involves training an algorithm with no prior information about the data. This algorithm categorizes the data into clusters. The most common unsupervised learning method is cluster analysis, which is used for exploratory data analysis to find hidden patterns or grouping in data.

From k-Nearest Neighbors to Support Vector Machines, and from Decision Trees to Neural Networks, each machine learning algorithm has its strengths and weaknesses, and it largely depends on the type of data and the business problem to be solved.

Predictive analytics is a vast field with diverse methods and models. These tools and concepts are simply instruments to the end goal: leveraging past patterns into insightful understanding to make better decisions about the future.

IV. The Power of Predictive Analytics: An Overview

1. Understanding Predictive Analytics

Predictive analytics is a branch of advanced analytics that uses data, statistical algorithms, and machine learning techniques to identify the probability of potential future outcomes based on historical data. The objective is to go beyond the information of what has happened in the past to deliver the best approximation of what will happen in the near future. This powerful tool brings together two separate but interconnected would-be data analysis techniques, predictive modeling and machine learning.

2. The Essence of Predictive Analytics

The essence of predictive analytics relies heavily upon capturing relationships between descriptive variables and predicted variables from previous events, and exploiting them to predict future outcomes. This process is beneficial in a wide array of fields, including internet marketing, financial services, insurance, telecommunications, travel, healthcare, pharmaceuticals, retail, and social media.

3. Predictive Analytics Process

The predictive analytics process is a series of steps that embraces both structured and unstructured data through various statistical, modeling, and machine learning algorithms to forecast future events. The process starts with defining the project followed by data collection. Later, data is subjected to analysis and transformed into a predictive model through techniques like regression and decision trees. This model is then deployed and monitored periodically to ensure it performs as expected.

4. Techniques in Predictive Analytics

Several techniques are used in predictive analytics; these include Machine Learning (ML), Artificial Neural Networks (ANN), Decision Trees, Regression, Time Series Analysis, and others. Each technique offers unique advantages and is suited to specific types of tasks, ranging from voting methods to non-linear predictive modeling.

5. Benefits of Predictive Analytics

Predictive analytics holds an assortment of benefits. For businesses, it aids in enhancing marketing campaigns, developing better products, and improving operations. It helps in detecting and preventing risks in sectors like cybersecurity and fraud management. It even plays a pivotal role in healthcare and lifesciences by helping doctors predict the likelihood of diseases, enhancing patient care, and aiding in drug discovery.

6. The Impact of Big Data on Predictive Analytics

The enormous volumes of data generated across multiple platforms have necessitated advancements in predictive analytics. Big data, with its three core elements – volume, velocity, and variety – provides a rich input source for predictive analytics, permitting in-depth insights for decision making.

7. Predictive Analytics and Business Intelligence

The amalgamation of predictive analytics and Business Intelligence (BI) tools aids organizations in leveraging their data for more informed decision-making. By applying BI tools to the predictive models, businesses can visualize data, track key performance metrics, and generate reports to streamline operations and increase profitability.

8. Challenges and Limitations of Predictive Analytics

Despite the numerous benefits, predictive analytics is not without limitations. The accuracy of results heavily depends on the quality of data. Misinterpreting data can lead to erroneous predictions. Moreover, maintaining data privacy and ensuring regulatory compliance also pose significant challenges.

9. The Future of Predictive Analytics

The future of predictive analytics is promising. The incorporation of AI and ML will make predictive models more precise. Real-time applications of predictive analytics are expected to increase, enabling instant decision-making and actions.

In the era of data-driven decisions, harnessing the power of predictive analytics enables organizations to look into the future and make proactive, data-driven decisions that lead to success.

IV.1 Understanding Predictive Analytics

Predictive analytics is the practice of extracting information from existing data sets in order to forecast future probabilities and trends. It is a statistical technique that includes an assortment of statistical algorithms, machine learning techniques, and analytical methods to identify the likelihood of future outcomes based on the data.

Predictive analytics revolves around the concept of harnessing the power of data in qualitative and quantitative forms. It performs this by identifying consistent patterns and associations in historical and transactional data to convert them into actionable decisions. Unlike traditional analytics, that only provide insights into what has happened, predictive analytics allows us to peer into the future and make well-informed decisions.

IV.2 Applications of Predictive Analytics

Predictive Analytics has a wide range of applications across various industries.

- **Marketing:** Companies use predictive models to foresee customer behavior and preferences. It helps in planning effective marketing strategies, improving acquisition, cross-selling, and retention.

- **Finance & Insurance:** They use it to identify fraudulent transactions and assess risk in loan underwriting. It aids in risk management by predicting the likely hood of a customer defaulting.
- **Healthcare:** Predictive analytics can estimate the probability of patients getting sick and predict hospital readmissions.
- **Manufacturing:** Predictive models can project inventory needs and predict machinery failures before they happen.

These applications are just the tip of the iceberg, predictive analytics has limitless potential in any field that deals with large amounts of data, which is growing exponentially these days.

IV.3 The Process of Predictive Analytics

The process of predictive analytics can be broken down into several basic steps:

1. Define the Project: The first step involves defining the project with a clear objective, project scope, and identifying the data sources.

2. Data Collection: This includes gathering relevant data from various sources which may include data warehouses, cloud data, or direct feeds.

3. Data Analysis: In this step, the collected data is statistically analyzed to detect trends, relations, and patterns that can be useful for predictive modelling

4. Model Building: Algorithms are built to predict future trends using the interpreted data.

5. Verification and Validation: The model is then tested and validated against known results to assess its accuracy and effectiveness.

6. Deployment: The validated model is then deployed to predict real-time or future outcomes.

7. Monitoring: The model's performance is consistently monitored to ensure it is providing the results as expected.

IV.4 Power of Predictive Analytics

Predictive analytics has revolutionized decision-making processes in businesses. It has rendered guesswork ineffective, paving the way for data-backed decisions. From sales forecasting to predictive maintenance, it has been used to optimize various processes.

With the power of predictive analytics, businesses can forecast future sales trends, understand customer behaviors, streamline operations, lessen risks, improve on marketing strategies, and deliver better servicing. It enables enterprises to become proactive, forward-looking, and performance-oriented.

However, as powerful predictive analytics might be, it doesn't overrule human judgement but reinforces it, by providing better and precise insights. It's important to understand that even the most accurate prediction isn't a guarantee but a well-calibrated estimate.

IV.5 Future of Predictive Analytics

Predictive analytics is expanding at a rapid pace with advancements in technologies like AI, machine learning, and big data. The future of predictive analytics looks promising as companies are increasingly using data for driving their strategies and making informed decisions. As more sectors understand the importance of predictive analytics, the range of its applications is expected to grow, making it an indispensable tool in the world powered by data.

Remember, predictive analytics is not a magic crystal ball that guarantees future outcomes, but, undoubtedly, it positions businesses better for future uncertainties by reducing risks and enabling effective decision-making.

The Basics and Importance of Predictive Analytics

Predictive Analytics is an advanced and dynamic analytical method. As a sharp contrast to traditional data analytics that analyze historical data, predictive analytics assumes a proactive approach and draws on the same data to predict future, unknown events. This approach offers remarkable possibilities for businesses as they can use these predictions to make better decisions, create proactive strategies, and gain a competitive edge.

Predictive analytics relies heavily on various techniques such as data mining, statistics, machine learning, and artificial intelligence to sift through current and historical data and predict what is likely to happen in the future. By doing so, it enables stakeholders to view future trends and behaviors, which could be crucial in a business scenario. The potential uses of predictive analytics extend across numerous industries such as healthcare, retail, finance, and public administration, among others.

Key Elements in Predictive Analytics

Predictive analytics is a complex process that requires a series of different but interconnected steps. At the heart of it all, the following elements play a vital role:

1. **Data Collection:** The accuracy and reliability of predictions highly depend on the quality and quantity of data available. Businesses need to collect as much relevant data as possible.
2. **Data Analysis:** This process analyzes and assesses the collected data, identifying patterns, relationships, and trends that might exist within the data.
3. **Statistical Analysis:** In this step, mathematicians apply statistical algorithms to the data to identify the different variables within it.
4. **Modeling:** The statistical analysis leads to creating models that reflect the potential future behavior of a data set.
5. **Deployment:** The models are used with fresh data to make predictions about future trends.
6. **Model Assessment:** Models are continually monitored and updated when necessary to keep the predictions as accurate as possible.

Harnessing the Power of Predictive Analytics

Predictive analytics holds powerful potential for businesses to drive revenue growth and optimize their operations. Here are some of the benefits that businesses can leverage when incorporating predictive analytics into their strategies:

1. **Improving Decision Making:** Predictive models help businesses make well-informed decisions based on insightful and accurate data. This approach improves the decision-making process by reducing guesswork and uncertainty.

2. **Anticipating Trends and Behavior:** It allows businesses to be proactive rather than reactive by anticipating market trends, consumer buying behavior, and foreseeing potential risks or opportunities.
3. **Boosting Operational Efficiency:** Predictive analytics can help optimize various business operations like inventory management, logistics, or workforce. By forecasting future demand or supply trends, companies can manage resources more efficiently.
4. **Enhancing Marketing Campaigns:** Marketers can leverage predictive analytics to better understand customer behavior and preferences, allowing them to create personalized marketing campaigns which are more likely to generate high conversion rates.
5. **Mitigating Risks:** Financial institutions can use predictive analytics to assess credit risks or the likelihood of a customer's loan default, thus improving their risk management capabilities.

In conclusion, predictive analytics offers businesses numerous possibilities to achieve their objectives and stay a step ahead in the market. By turning data into predictive insights, they can unlock unforeseeable growth and value. Despite its complexities, the rich benefits it offers make it a wiser choice, making predictive analytics a quintessential tool in today's business landscape. As more businesses harness the power of predictive analytics, we can look forward to radical transformations in various sectors.

IV.1 Understanding the Essence of Predictive Analytics

Predictive analytics is a branch of advanced analytics that leverages a multitude of technological tools and statistical techniques, such as machine learning and predictive modeling, to make predictions about unknown future events in any given domain. The purpose of predictive analytics is not just to understand what has happened or what is currently happening, but more significantly, to foresee what might happen next.

Predictive analytics stands on three important pillars: data, statistical algorithms, and machine learning techniques. It sifts through massive amounts of data, drawing from various sources like current and historical data, and combines it with statistical algorithms and machine learning techniques to identify the odds of future outcomes. Once deciphered, the data-driven predictions enable organizations to validate assumptions or pose new questions about the future, assisting in proactive decision-making and strategizing.

The real power of predictive analytics lies in its ability to provide actionable insights based on data. By leveraging predictive analytics, organizations can anticipate emerging trends, predict user behavior, estimate potential risks, and unlock insights to drive business strategies, fostering a forward-looking approach. Notably, predictive analytics not only identifies possibilities but also pinpoints the level of certainty in its predictions, empowering organizations to make more informed, data-driven decisions.

IV.2 Scope and Impact of Predictive Analytics

Predictive Analytics has wide applicability across several industrial sectors, including healthcare, finance, retail, travel, telecommunication, energy, and more, strategically shaping their operations and decision-making processes.

In healthcare, for instance, predictive analytics can be used to predict disease outbreaks and patient readmissions, thus allowing for better healthcare planning and administration.

Similarly, in finance and retail, organizations use predictive analytics to evaluate consumer buying habits, forecast demand, minimize risk, and enhance customer experience.

Besides operational optimization, predictive analytics is instrumental in identifying risks and fraud. Through anomaly detection and network analysis, it can spot out irregularities, unusual patterns, or suspicious activities, providing critical benefits in sectors like banking, insurance, cybersecurity, and even government entities.

Moreover, predictive analytics also plays a key role in managing resources. By predicting demand, organizations can optimize inventory, thereby significantly reducing costs. Likewise, in human resource management, predictive analytics helps in identifying the traits of successful employees, enabling smarter, more effective hiring.

IV.3 The Evolution of Predictive Analytics

The scope of predictive analytics has vastly expanded with the advent of Big Data and improved processing technologies. Today, predictive analytics is part of a larger system - Business Intelligence (BI). Together with descriptive and prescriptive analytics, predictive analytics offers organizations a 360-degree understanding of their operations and the business environment, shaping a data-centric business model.

Going forward, the increasing integration of Artificial Intelligence (AI) and Machine Learning (ML) is set to further enhance the accuracy and speed of predictions, thus strengthening the role of predictive analytics in decision-making and strategy planning.

IV.4 Challenges & Future of Predictive Analytics

While predictive analytics offers vast benefits, it also brings challenges, such as data privacy and security, data quality and integration, and the implementation of results. Addressing these issues demands strategic planning and changing business culture.

Nevertheless, the future of predictive analytics looks promising. As organizations continue to venture deeper into the data-driven universe, the reliance on predictive analytics will undoubtedly intensify. Bolder technological advancements in fields such as AI, ML, and cloud computing will continue to enrich predictive analytics, rendering it a cornerstone of futurist, data-centric business models, and society at large.

IV.1 Understanding Predictive Analytics

Predictive analytics is a method that utilizes statistical algorithms and machine learning techniques to assess historical data, predict future outcomes, and understand potential future trends. It is an aspect of data analytics geared towards making predictions about unseen or unobserved future events.

This approach relies on capturing relationships between explanatory variables and the metric variables they're considering for future predictions. These captures happen through the use of models, which are constructed from historical data. Once a predictive model is built, it can be applied to current data to predict what will happen next.

Predictive analytics can yield immense benefits across varied industries, ranging from healthcare and marketing to finance and retail. They enable organizations to create forecasts that can help them shape their strategic actions and decisions.

IV.1.1 The Four Stages of Predictive Analytics

1. **Data Collection:** This is the process of gathering raw data from various sources, which could include databases, data warehouses, or external third-party sources. This raw data sets the foundation for further analysis and predictions.
2. **Data Analysis:** Once the data is collected, the next step is to clean, process and analyze the data. The goal is to discover patterns or trends that could provide useful insight into future outcomes.
3. **Statistical Analysis:** This third stage involves creating a predictive model based on the data that's been gathered and analyzed. It uses algorithms, probability, and statistical methods to develop a model that could be used to make predictions.
4. **Predictive Modeling:** The final stage of predictive analytics involves using the predictive model to make predictions about future outcomes. This process helps organizations make informed business decisions.

IV.1.2 Tools and techniques used in Predictive Analytics

Several tools are used in predictive analytics to deal with vast amounts of data and complex algorithms. Software platforms like R, Python, SPSS, and SAS offer features for data manipulation, visualization and algorithm implementation necessary for predictive analytics.

Moreover, techniques used in predictive analytics include linear regressions, logistic regressions, decision trees, and neural networks. The nature of the data, the industry, and the objective of the prediction determine the choice of these techniques.

IV.1.3 Applications of Predictive Analytics

Its potential ranges far across a wide array of industries where rich data is produced. For example, in healthcare, predictive analytics could provide early diagnoses and treatment of diseases. In finance, it could assist in predicting stock price movements or evaluate credit risk.

The retail sector uses it to predict customer behavior and adapt their strategies to boost sales. The marketing industry uses it to predict the efficiency of marketing campaigns and make necessary alterations to improve outcomes.

Despite the challenges in data quality and the skill required to interpret and utilize data effectively, with the right tools and skilled staff, predictive analytics can provide key insights that can drive a business forward. It's a potent tool that has reshaped several industries and, with the advent of big data and more advanced algorithms, it continues to expand its realm of influence.

It's important to remember, though, that predictive analytics is not about predicting the "future," but estimating potential outcomes. Its objective is not to deliver absolute and deterministic predictions but to give users enough information to assess what their next action should be. It reduces the realm of uncertainty, thereby enabling businesses to maneuver wisely and capitalize on future opportunities.

V. Role of Predictive Analytics in Various Industries

5.1 The Impact of Predictive Analytics in the Healthcare Industry

Predictive analytics has been increasingly important in the healthcare sector, helping providers predict patient outcomes, manage treatments, and make better-informed decisions. It is applied in a wide range of areas including disease management, hospital management, patient satisfaction, and healthcare policy-making.

Healthcare providers use predictive analytics to identify individuals who are at risk of chronic diseases like diabetes and heart disease. They use data collected from electronic health records, laboratory tests, and physical examinations to forecast individual disease risks. As a result, doctors can intervene early and take preventive measures, improving patient health outcome and reducing healthcare costs.

Moreover, predictive analytics is also used in hospital management. It helps predict patient admission rates, enabling hospitals to optimize staff allocation, reduce patient waiting time, and improve healthcare delivery. It also helps forecast patient readmission, which is crucial for resource planning and reducing hospital readmission penalties.

In addition, healthcare organizations also use predictive analytics to enhance patient satisfaction. They analyze patient satisfaction surveys, online reviews, and social media posts to identify factors that contribute to patient satisfaction. By addressing issues that cause dissatisfaction, healthcare providers can improve patient experience and foster patient loyalty.

Predictive analytics also plays a crucial role in healthcare policy-making. Policymakers use predictive models to estimate the effect of policy changes on healthcare delivery and outcomes, helping them make better healthcare decisions. They can evaluate the cost-effectiveness of different healthcare interventions and devise policies that maximize healthcare benefits and minimize costs.

5.2 Powering Financial Services with Predictive Analytics

Predictive analytics has emerged as a game-changer in the financial services industry as well. From predicting market trends to managing risks, predictive analytics provides a competitive advantage to financial institutions by helping them make data-driven decisions.

Investment firms use predictive analytics to forecast market trends. They analyze economic data, company performance metrics, and news feeds to predict stock prices and make investment decisions. Today, many firms use automated trading algorithms that rely on predictive analytics to execute trades in real-time.

Additionally, predictive analytics is used extensively in credit scoring. Banks and credit card companies analyze an individual's financial history to predict their likelihood of default. The predictions help companies decide whether to approve a loan application and set interest rates.

Risk management is another area where predictive analytics is used in the financial sector. Financial institutions use predictive models to forecast portfolio risks and devise suitable risk mitigation strategies. In insurance, predictive analytics is used to calculate insurance premiums based on the applicant's risk profile, improving the profitability of insurance policies.

5.3 Predictive Analytics in Retail and E-commerce

Predictive analytics has also reshaped the retail and e-commerce industry. It helps businesses forecast consumer demand, optimize supply chain, personalize customer experience, and improve profitability.

Retailers utilize predictive analytics to forecast consumer demand for different products. They analyze historical sales data, current trends, and market research to ensure optimal stock levels. With accurate demand forecasting, retailers can avoid stockouts and overstocks, reducing inventory costs and improving customer satisfaction.

Predictive analytics also plays a critical role in supply chain management. It helps predict delays in supply chain and devise contingency plans, ensuring streamlined operations and on-time deliveries.

Moreover, predictive analytics is used to personalize customer experience. Retailers analyze customer behavior, purchase history, and feedback to predict their product preferences and shopping habits. They then use these insights to personalize marketing messages and product recommendations, improving customer engagement and boosting sales.

Finally, predictive analytics helps retailers improve profitability. By analyzing sales data, product costs, and other financial metrics, retailers can predict profitability of different products and make data-driven pricing and promotion decisions, maximizing their ROI.

5.4 Harnessing Predictive Analytics in Manufacturing

The adoption of predictive analytics in the manufacturing sector has paved the way for significant advancements. It enables manufacturers to predict machine failures, optimize production processes, manage supply chain, and make informed business decisions.

Predictive maintenance is one of the key applications of predictive analytics in manufacturing. Manufacturers analyze sensor data from machinery to predict equipment failures and schedule maintenance activities, reducing downtime and maintenance costs.

Furthermore, predictive analytics helps optimize the manufacturing process. By analyzing production data, manufacturers can forecast production outputs, identify bottlenecks, and improve efficiency. It can also help in quality control by predicting product defects and enabling timely corrective actions.

Predictive analytics is also used in supply chain management. Manufacturers analyze historical data and current trends to forecast supply and demand, enabling them to manage inventory, plan production, and ensure timely deliveries.

Lastly, predictive analytics aids business decision-making. Manufacturers can analyze sales data, market trends, and financial metrics to make decisions on product pricing, market entry, and business expansion.

5.5 Predictive Analytics Driving the Future of Education Sector

Predictive Analytics is making strides in the education sector as well. Right from predicting student performance to enhancing the teaching process, and optimizing operational efficiency, it is transforming the way the education sector functions.

Institutions are increasingly using predictive analytics to predict student performance. By analyzing student attendance, engagement metrics, and past performance data, educators can identify students at risk of underperforming or dropping out. Early identification allows for timely intervention which can help improve student outcomes and reduce dropout rates.

Also, predictive analytics is being used to inform and enhance teaching methodologies. For instance, educators can use data to understand what teaching styles and strategies are most effective and adapt their teaching practices accordingly, improving student learning experiences.

Predictive analytics also assists in operational tasks like streamlining the admission process. Institutions can use predictive models to understand which applicants are likely to accept admission offers, ensuring efficient resource allocation. Additionally, forecasting trends in enrollment can help institutions strategize future academic offerings and infrastructure planning.

To sum up, with the power of predictive analytics, these diverse industries are leveraging data to forecast future trends, optimize their operations, and make strategic decisions. By harnessing the power of predictive analytics, these industries are not only improving their efficiency and effectiveness, but also gaining a competitive advantage in the marketplace.

A. Healthcare

Predictive analytics holds a very significant role in the healthcare industry. Health care professionals use predictive analytics to predict epidemics, cure disease, improve the quality of life, and avoid preventable deaths. With the volume of health data increasing at a very rapid rate, predictive analytics can help in making sense of this data and provide actionable insights.

Predictive analysis in healthcare can involve the prediction of diseases, patients who are close to suffering from any type of illness, prediction of when a disease might occur, assistance in the examination of the patient's health, decision about clinical processes, and regular patient health monitoring. This approach provides faster disease diagnosis, improved patient outcomes, cost-effective treatments, and improved quality of care.

For example, using historical data about the progression of a particular disease in patients with similar genetic makeup and lifestyle, healthcare professionals can predict how a disease will progress in a new patient. This information can be used to personalize treatment for each patient, ultimately leading to better health outcomes.

B. Retail

Another industry where predictive analytics plays a crucial role is retail. Retailers use predictive analytics to understand their customers better, predict customer behaviors, optimize pricing, planning and forecasting inventory, and managing the supply chain.

Retailers use predictive analytics to anticipate the needs and wants of their customers and personalize their experience with the goal of increasing sales and consumer loyalty. For example, predictive analytics can be used to analyze a customer's past purchases and browsing behavior to recommend products that they are likely to be interested in.

Moreover, predictive analytics enables retailers to optimize their inventory by accurately predicting the demand for various products at different times. This led to fewer stockouts and overstocks, ultimately reducing costs and increasing customer satisfaction.

C. Finance and Banking

In the banking and financial sector, predictive analytics is deployed in risk assessment, fraud detection, marketing, customer retention and serves in improving overall customer experience. Banks use predictive models to predict the likelihood of default for individual loans, to determine your credit risk score. Banks also implement predictive analytics in their workflows to detect unusual behavior that could indicate fraudulent activity.

Investment firms frequently use predictive analytics to forecast market trends and to inform their investment strategies. By analyzing historical market data, firms can make informed predictions about future market movements and adjust their investment strategies accordingly.

D. Manufacturing

Manufacturing companies use predictive analytics to forecast demand, plan for production, operational efficiency, reduce costs, manage supply chains, and maintain the quality.

Predictive maintenance is also a major application of predictive analytics in manufacturing. Companies can predict when a piece of equipment is likely to fail, and they can perform maintenance in advance to prevent costly downtime.

E. Telecommunications

In the telecommunications industry, predictive analytics aids in customer segmentation, reducing customer churn, predictive maintenance, optimizing network quality, and improving customer experience.

In a bid to reduce churn, telecom companies can predict which customers are likely to switch to a different carrier to take proactive steps to retain those customers. Also, expected demand can be forecasted leading to smart capacity planning and network optimization.

F. Energy and Utilities

Predictive analytics has also made significant strides in the energy sector. Energy companies use these tools to forecast demand, optimize grid performance, predict equipment failures, and to make informed decisions about energy production.

Predictive analytics enables utilities to manage their resources more effectively by predicting consumption patterns. It can also help in identifying potential problems before a failure occurs, reducing downtime and maintenance costs.

Each of these industries has its unique set of challenges that predictive analytics can address. Thus, the potential of predictive analytics to improve decision-making, reduce costs, and optimize performance is immense and industries across the spectrum can benefit from it. The key to harnessing the power of predictive analytics lies in understanding what questions to ask, what data to use, and how to interpret the results.

Predictive Analytics in Healthcare: A Revolutionary Approach

The healthcare industry represents one of the most vital sectors where predictive analytics can play a revolutionary role. The massive amounts of data generated in healthcare - from patient records to complex genetic information - present enormous potential for predictive analysis.

Enhanced Patient Care

Firstly, predictive analytics can significantly improve patient care. It can help clinicians predict risk factors for diseases, enabling earlier interventions that could prevent severe health issues. For instance, by analyzing a patient's medical history, lifestyle habits, and genetic factors, an algorithm could predict their likelihood of developing a chronic illness, such as diabetes or heart disease. Armed with this insight, physicians can tailor preventive measures and treatments to the patient's individual needs, from recommending lifestyle modifications to starting pharmaceutical therapies.

Improved Operational Efficiency

Optimizing operational efficiency is another advantage healthcare institutions can gain from predictive analytics. Hospitals generate a vast amount of data from their operational activities, such as patient admission rates, equipment usage, staff schedules, and their supply chains. Analyzing this data can unveil patterns and trends that can help administrators improve resource allocation, reduce waste, increase patient satisfaction, and ultimately, boost the overall efficiency of the healthcare system.

Informed Decision-Making

Additionally, predictive analytics can guide healthcare policymakers and administrators in making informed decisions. By predicting future healthcare trends, including disease outbreaks and healthcare demand, policymakers can adequately prepare for these scenarios and create effective strategies. For instance, during the COVID-19 pandemic, predictive analytics was used to forecast infection rates, which guided decisions on lockdown measures, hospital resource allocation, and vaccine distribution.

Drug Development and Personalized Medicine

Moreover, predictive analytics can transform the pharmaceutical sector by streamlining drug development and paving the way for personalized medicine. Through the analysis of clinical trial data, the duration, cost and success rate of developing new drugs can be significantly improved. Meanwhile, by examining patient genetic information and their responses to certain medications, custom treatments with the highest likelihood of success can be established, minimizing side effects and enhancing survival rates.

Mental Health Predictions

Predictive analytics also extends its benefits to the mental health field. Mental health illnesses such as depression, anxiety, and schizophrenia can be challenging to diagnose accurately. Through predictive analytics, powering machine learning algorithms with historical patient data can identify patterns that may forecast mental health conditions and allow for early, potentially life-saving interventions.

Predictive analytics can undoubtedly drive considerable improvements to the healthcare industry's many facets. However, privacy and ethical considerations must always be at the forefront of implementing any data-driven solutions in healthcare. As we continue to harness the power of data for future insights, securing patients' trust and maintaining their dignity must remain paramount.

5.1 Healthcare

The role of predictive analytics in healthcare cannot be understated. It has transformed the idea of personalized medicine into a reality by promoting data-driven clinical decision-making, improving patient experiences, and reducing healthcare costs. In particular, predictive modeling has facilitated the identification of high-risk patient populations, oftentimes in relation to serious chronic diseases such as heart disease, diabetes, and cancer.

Through the application of predictive analytics, healthcare administrators can analyze Electronic Health Records (EHRs), medical imaging data, genetic data, and even health-related social media data to stratify risk. This is of immense value to healthcare providers, given that 5% of the patient population typically accounts for about 50% of healthcare costs. Identifying these patients before adverse events occur could not only save lives but huge costs too.

Moreover, healthcare organizations are increasingly leveraging predictive analytics to ensure efficient resource allocation. For instance, managing the ebb and flow of patient admissions to ensure optimal occupancy and staffing levels. The application of predictive analytics in hospital readmissions has also begun to gain traction - the ability to predict which patients are at an increased risk of returning to a hospital within 30 days of their discharge could significantly reduce readmission rates and corresponding penalties.

5.2 Retail

The retail industry has been one of the earliest adopters of predictive analytics, with many organizations understanding the potential that lies within the billions of data points that they collect. In essence, predictive analytics helps retailers in understanding and predicting customer behavior. This predictive power can inform a variety of strategic decisions such as what products to stock, which ones to discount, how to personalize offers, and even when to send marketing messages.

Equipped with historic transaction data, demographic data, and social media behavior data, retailers can predict future trends, conduct market basket analysis, and more. This not only helps in delivering a personalized shopping experience for their customers but also increases operational efficiency and profitability.

One of the most popular use-cases of predictive analytics in retail is in demand forecasting. By accurately predicting the demand for different products at different times and locations, retailers can optimize inventory levels, reduce stock-outs and overstocks, and increase turn-over rates.

5.3 Finance

In the finance sector, predictive analytics is being used to assess credit risk, detect fraudulent transactions, maximise cross-selling and up-selling, predict stock performance, and optimize trading strategies.

Risk assessment is potentially one of the most valuable applications of predictive analytics in this sector. Financial institutions can utilize predictive models to score and rank potential borrowers on their likelihood of defaulting on a loan payment, thereby improving their ability to mitigate risk and decrease losses.

In the area of fraud detection, predictive analytics can identify patterns and abnormalities that could suggest fraudulent behavior, thereby preventing losses before they occur. Additionally, predictive analytics can inform investment strategies by forecasting market trends and providing insight into future performance based on historical data.

5.4 Manufacturing

The manufacturing sector has traditionally been reactive when it comes to maintenance - machines are repaired or replaced after they have failed. Predictive analytics has the potential to turn this paradigm around with the help of predictive maintenance. This involves using sensor data to predict equipment failures before they occur, allowing time for preventative action. This shift not only increases operational efficiency but also results in significant cost savings, as unplanned downtime in manufacturing can be exceedingly expensive.

Predictive analytics can also add value to the manufacturing process by optimizing the supply chain. From forecasting demand, managing inventory, to route planning, predictive analytics can increase efficiency, lower costs, and even reduce the environmental impact.

Privacy implications, affordability constraints, stakeholder buy-in, and data quality are among the challenges that exist in applying predictive analytics across industries. However, the potential benefits far outweigh these challenges. Undeniably, predictive analytics is a powerful tool that can drive insights and operational efficiencies across a broad range of sectors.

V.1. Predictive Analytics in Healthcare Industry

Healthcare represents a significant sector where the application of predictive analytics has dramatically changed the way care is delivered. Hospitals, clinics, and other healthcare providers use predictive models to identify the probability of certain patient outcomes and make more informed decisions based on this data.

Preventive Care and Chronic Disease Management

Predictive analytics has been particularly useful in preventive care and disease management, especially for chronic conditions such as diabetes, heart disease, and cancer. By analyzing patient data from electronic health records, genetic tests, and lifestyle factors, predictive models can identify patients who are at high risk of developing these illnesses. Healthcare providers can then take proactive measures to mitigate these risks, such as offering personalized health advice and adjustments to treatment plans.

Patient Re-admissions

Hospitals encounter substantial costs, both financial and quality of care, associated with patient re-admissions. Predictive analytics can flag patients at high risk of readmission, allowing hospitals to implement resource-intensive interventions in a targeted manner, thereby reducing unnecessary re-admissions effectively and efficiently.

Hospital Resource Management

Predictive analytics is also playing a pivotal role in managing hospital resources and optimizing operations. For instance, predictive models can forecast patient flow, helping hospitals manage everything from bed occupancy to scheduling surgeries. It helps healthcare facilities reduce waiting times, improve patient satisfaction, and better allocate resources.

Drug Discovery and Development

In the pharmaceutical industry, predictive analytics is being used extensively to accelerate drug discovery and development. By analyzing a combination of genetic, clinical and pharmacological data, predictive models can highlight potential therapeutic targets and predict how different individuals will respond to a drug. This approach is not only faster and less costly but can also improve patient outcomes by identifying the most effective and safe drugs.

V.2. Predictive Analytics in the Financial Industry

The financial industry has been a major adopter of predictive analytics, using it to assess risks, identify fraudulent activities, enhance customer relationships, and improve performance.

Risk Management

Financial institutions like banks and insurance companies first and foremost use predictive models to assess and manage risk. Key profiles such as credit scoring and insurance underwriting rely heavily on analytics to make informed decisions. Predictive models help identify potential loan defaulters in the future by analyzing various factors like payment history, credit usage, and other related indicators.

Fraud Detection

Predictive analytics plays a critical role in identifying fraudulent activities in real time. By combining various tracking data through algorithms, institutions can identify potential anomalies or suspicious transactions and immediately flag them for investigation, potentially saving billions of dollars lost due to fraud.

Performance Improvement

Financial performance can be significantly improved by employing predictive analytics. Predictive models can help portfolio managers make more informed decisions by anticipating market trends and investor behavior. It also aids traders through algorithmic trading, utilizing historic and real-time data to predict profitable trading opportunities.

V.3. Predictive Analytics in the Retail Industry

The retail industry is another major sector that leverages predictive analytics to understand customer behavior and optimize business strategies.

Inventory Management

Predictive analytics can offer very accurate projections about how much of a specific product will sell, taking into account variables such as seasonality, trends, and economic indicators. This allows retailers to manage their inventory

more effectively, reducing wastage due to overstocking or
lost sales due to understocking.

Personalized Marketing

Predictive analytics aids retailers in understanding the
shopping behavior and preferences of their customers. By
analyzing data from past purchases and online browsing
habits, predictive models can also forecast future buying
behavior. This personalized approach to marketing not only
enhances customer experience but also increases sales and
customer loyalty.

These are just a few examples illustrating the role of
predictive analytics in various industries. The potential use
cases are nearly infinite, and as technology continues to
evolve, its application will only continue to expand. Predictive
analytics is no longer a luxury but a necessity for any
business looking to stay competitive in today's data-driven
world.

VI. Case Studies: Successful Use of Predictive Analytics

Case Study 1: Netflix's Evolving Machine Learning

Netflix, the streaming behemoth, carries the distinction of
being one of the most notable early adopters of predictive
analytics. Netflix is a standout example of not just simply
implementing predictive analytics, but effectively evolving it
to enhance customer satisfaction and user experience all
while increasing revenue.

In 2006, Netflix launched the "Netflix Prize", offering $1 million to anyone who could help them to improve the accuracy of their movie recommendation engine by 10%. It was a wake-up call about the company's sharp turns into understanding its viewers' preferences and providing them with what they exactly want.

Netflix's primary use of predictive analytics is its advanced recommendation engine. Algorithms analyze customer's data, historical viewing habits, and is compared to the hundreds of thousands of other user's data to suggest content that the user may enjoy. This enables Netflix to retain subscribers by consistently providing them with content they find appealing.

Tailored content creation based on predictive analytics is another way that Netflix uses this technology. One outstanding example is the creation of the popular series, House of Cards. Netflix decided to invest a whopping $100m for two seasons after their predictive analytics showed that users who loved the British version of the show also adored Kevin Spacey and David Fincher.

The predictive analytics model also accounts for Netflix's regional content customization. With its treasure of worldwide user data, Netflix identifies the trends popular among different regions and curates its content accordingly. This allows them to reach wide-ranging audiences and increasing the stickiness of the platform.

The success of Netflix's use of predictive analytics is demonstrated not only in its impressive subscriber count of over 200 million, but also in its competitive edge over other media streaming platforms. It effectively showcases the power and potential of predictive analytics when used optimally, providing personalized experiences to consumers, and fostering their loyalty.

Case Study 2: American Express Identifying High-quality Customers

American Express, one of the world's largest credit card companies, uses predictive analytics to identify and target high-potential customers. Their predictive analytics model helps them understand the behavior of their customers, their spending habits, creditworthiness, even predicting future loyalty.

One instance of their predictive analytics use is the creation of a sophisticated predictive model that analyzes historical transactions and identifies patterns associated with fake charges. The model enables them to predict if a new transaction, whether it be from an existing or new customer, is fraudulent. This reduces their risk exposure significantly and improves their service to genuine customers.

Another use has been for customer retention. American Express uses predictive analytics to identify customers who have been loyal to the company, maintained a good credit history, and regularly spend with their credit card. They then offer exclusive deals, privileges, and benefits to these customers enhancing their satisfaction and reducing churn.

The success of the predictive analytics model by American Express is another testament to the immense potential of predictive analytics. Their successful targeting and retaining of high-quality customers, risk mitigation tactics, and ability to distinguish fraudulent activities has given them a significant competitive advantage in the credit card industry.

Case Study 3: Google's Flu Trends: Predicting Public Health

In 2008, Google launched an initiative called Google Flu Trends (GFT) to monitor the spread of flu by mining search query data. They used big data accumulated from search terms related to the flu, to predict flu outbreaks faster than the traditional systems used by health organizations like The Centers for Disease Control and Prevention (CDC).

Though GFT had its struggles and controversy, and ultimately was stopped in 2015, it opened the world to the potential use of predictive analytics in providing insights on public health. The idea of using real-time, easily accessible data, to monitor and predict the rise and spread of illnesses has spurred advancements in this field and led to a plethora of companies and organizations utilizing similar methods for disease prediction and prevention.

These case studies portray the vast potential of predictive analytics in varied industries revealing trends, mitigating risks, improving services, personalizing content, and preventing diseases. As businesses continue to collect and analyze more data, it is clear that predictive analytics techniques will become even more pivotal to business success.

VI.A Case Study: Amazon and Predictive Analytics

Amazon, a global e-commerce specialist, is a great example of the application of predictive analytics for outstanding business results. Amazon uses predictive analytics to recommend products to its hundreds of millions of users worldwide, leading to higher user satisfaction, increased sales, and continuous business growth.

VI.A.1 Data Collection and Management

Amazon has multi-dimensional data that include information about customer buying habits, search patterns on its website, wish lists, shopping carts, returns, and even how long users spend hovering their cursors over certain items. They gather big data from every customer interaction, across multiple platforms and touchpoints. This data is then categorized, stored, and processed in vast cloud-based systems, ensuring its availability for in-depth analysis.

VI.A.2 Product Recommendations

Amazon extensively uses predictive analytics to provide personalized product recommendations. When a customer logs in, predictive models run real-time analysis of the customer's data against a database of products, creating a personalized list of products that are likely to appeal to them. This not only helps in enhancing customer satisfaction but also increases their cart value.

VI.A.3 Inventory Management

Amazon also applies predictive analytics in managing inventory. They analyse data related to purchase history, current trends, seasonality etc. to forecast demand for various products. Based on this, they balance their stock in different warehouses. This greatly helps in reducing costs related to overstocking and lost sales due to understocking.

VI.A.4 Fraud Detection

In the e-commerce industry, fraudulent transactions are a major concern. Amazon uses predictive analytics to detect fraudulent activities. By comparing current transaction data with historical fraudulent patterns, their models help identify potentially fraudulent transactions, thereby minimizing losses and ensuring consumer trust.

VI.A.5 Enhancing User Experience

Amazon also uses predictive analytics to enhance user experience on their website. They analyse user behavior data like clickstream, search history, page dwell time, etc. Using this data, they personalize website design, product placements and promotional messages for individual users.

VI.A.6 Conclusion

By harnessing the power of predictive analytics, Amazon has revolutionized the e-commerce industry. The deep insights generated from predictive analytics have significantly reduced costs, maximized profits, and greatly improved customer satisfaction. This case study highlights the vast potential of predictive analytics when implemented correctly with a strategic vision.

This case also underscores that harnessing the power of predictive analytics not only requires a huge amount of data but also the right tools to analyze this data and develop valuable insights. It is evident that investing in predictive analytics can be highly profitable for businesses, but it requires a deep understanding of the field and a strategic approach to implementation.

The Amazon case study is not a unique case in the use of predictive analytics. In the subsequent subsections, we will look at other businesses that have capitalized on predictive analytics for remarkable success in their respective industries.

Stay tuned to discover how other industry leaders are harnessing the power of predictive analytics!

Case Study 1: Netflix- Predictive Analytics for Personalized Recommendations

One of the most successful and illustrative examples of utilizing predictive analytics comes from the online streaming giant, Netflix. Netflix's success can be largely attributed to its use of predictive analytics to deliver personalized content recommendations to its 200 million users around the globe.

Netflix uses a predictive model that analyzes hundreds of billions of data points every day. This model combines explicit data provided by the user, such as their viewing history and ratings, with implicit data, such as browsing behavior and viewing habits, to predict what a user wants to watch next before they even know it themselves.

Using Predictive Analytics

Netflix's analytics engine doesn't use traditional demography or geography to offer recommendations. Instead, it clusters users based on their viewing taste, irrespective of their location. The algorithm keeps learning and refining its predictions with every interaction and data point. Netflix even uses predictive analytics to decide which film and series to produce. For instance, data suggested that a significant overlap of subscribers who loved political dramas also favored Oscar-nominated actor Kevin Spacey and director David Fincher. As such, Netflix green-lighted the production of a political drama, "House of Cards" featuring both Spacey and Fincher that became a huge success.

The use of predictive analytics helped Netflix to reduce its churn rates significantly, by ensuring that users always find the content they're interested in, without wasting much time browsing. This also leads to customer satisfaction and higher viewing hours, directly enhancing Netflix's revenue.

The Impact

Netflix's application of predictive analytics is not just about recommending the right content - it's about sustaining and increasing engagement over time. It is estimated that the company saves1 billion dollars per year as a result of its personalized recommendation engine.

Additionally, the use of predictive analytics in content production decision-making has also reaped positive results for Netflix. Shows such as "House of Cards" and "Orange is the New Black" were commissioned based on insights derived from predictive models, and they gained massive popularity, attracting millions of new subscribers.

Lessons Learned

This case study offers several insights that can be applied across different sectors:

1. **Enhanced Customer Experience**: Predictive analytics can significantly enhance the user experience by delivering personalized and targeted content. A better experience leads to higher customer retention and lower churn rates.
2. **Data-Driven Decision-Making**: The use of predictive analytics for decision-making can lead to more

accurate and efficient decisions, potentially saving resources and cost by minimizing risks associated with intuitive decision-making.

3. **Continuous Learning**: Predictive models are not static - they learn and improve with every additional data point, ensuring that predictions are refined and updated over time.

In conclusion, Netflix's successful use of predictive analytics demonstrates the power of data and how it can be harnessed to not only exceed customer expectations but also guide strategic business decisions.

Case Study 1: Starbucks - Tailoring Customer Experience with Predictive Analytics

Starbucks, one of the world's most popular coffeehouse chains, is an excellent example of a company that effectively utilizes predictive analytics to enhance its customer experience.

Understanding Customer Preferences

The initial step Starbucks took in leveraging its data was to launch 'Starbucks Rewards', a loyalty program that encourages customers to make purchases in exchange for reward points. This program encompassed a mobile app that has been downloaded over 19 million times, according to a report from BI Intelligence. In completing transactions through this system, customers produced a significant amount of consensual data about their purchase history and behavior.

As Starbucks collected and analyzed this data, they were able to better understand each individual customer's preferences, such as their preferred drinks, food, and store locations, as well as the frequency and time of their visits.

Implementing Predictive Models

Once Starbucks obtained a clear understanding of their customer behaviors, they developed predictive models that enabled them to anticipate future customer behavior based on historical data.

By analyzing patterns and trends in the data, Starbucks' predictive models can provide insights such as which new products are likely to be successful, what kind of promotional offers would drive customer interest, and how changes in price or store availability can affect sales.

This allowed Starbucks to make data-driven decisions about product development, marketing strategies, and inventory management, thereby enhancing their operational efficiency and profitability.

Personalization through Predictive Analytics

The predictive analytics model could also estimate the probability of a specific customer buying a particular item at a certain time or location, allowing Starbucks to deliver a highly personalized customer experience.

Starbucks used these insights to personalize their marketing campaigns, delivering individualized offers directly to customers through their mobile app. Further, the data was used to personalize the customer experience in their physical store locations, ensuring that popular items were always available to customers, while less popular items could be phased out or replaced.

The Success Story

Starbucks' use of predictive analytics turned data into actionable insights, allowing the company to stay ahead in a competitive market. It has helped build customer loyalty, increase sales, and drive growth.

In a presentation for investors, Starbucks' CFO Patrick Grismer stated that their targeted marketing efforts, driven by predictive analytics, contributed to a whopping 2% increase in comparable US store sales in the second quarter of 2019.

The Starbucks case study noticeably demonstrates how predictive analytics can help businesses understand customer behavior on a granular level, predict future trends, improve operations, and tailor a personalized customer experience.

Conclusion

Evidently, Starbucks' successful utilization of predictive analytics serves as an excellent case study for companies seeking to harness the power of data for future insights. It shows how businesses can use predictive analytics models to drive customer loyalty, reduce waste, and increase sales. This valuable lesson can be applicable to companies in other sectors as well, making predictive analytics an indispensable tool in the data-driven business world.

Case Study 1: Coca-Cola and the Power of Predictive Analytics

Throughout its journey to become a world-renowned brand, Coca-Cola has always embraced cutting-edge technology to improve its business operations. Most recently, this technological renaissance has taken the form of a deep dive into predictive analytics, allowing Coca-Cola to understand its customers on a granular level.

The Problem

Growing a business is an inherently challenging process, and Coca-Cola faced several formidable hurdles. First, the vast size of the customer base made it difficult to parse through the magnitude of existing customer data. Furthermore, keeping track of changing customer preferences for different products was no easy task. Without the right solutions, these problems could hinder Coca-Cola's growth and reduce its competitiveness in an intensively competitive global market.

The Solution

To overcome these challenges, Coca-Cola turned to predictive analytics to dissect their dense cascade of consumer data. By leveraging machine learning algorithms and data analytics, the company began predicting trends in consumer behavior, thereby making informed decisions.

To start the process, Coca-Cola gathered past customer data, including historical buying patterns, seasonality of purchases, and response to previous marketing campaigns.

They also collected data on demographic factors such as age, gender, and location. These datasets were then fed into machine learning algorithms to create predictive models.

For instance, in one of their projects, Coca-Cola used predictive analytics to forecast orange crop yields. This helped the company manage its orange juice production efficiently, minimizing waste and improving cost-effectiveness.

The Implementation

The implementation of predictive analytics within Coca-Cola required a shift in the company's approach to data. The transformation involved both a cultural shift - with the company embracing data-driven decision-making - and technological shift - with the use of advanced machine learning algorithms and analytical tools.

Investing in building in-house data analytic talent was key to this transformation. Coca-Cola trained its technical staff in drawing insights from data and implementing predictive models. It further collaborated with external partners for advanced expertise.

The Results

Thanks to predictive analytics, Coca-Cola managed to derive an unprecedented level of insights from their consumer data. The predictive models helped the company get a granular understanding of its customer's tastes, enabling the delivery of personalized marketing campaigns.

Furthermore, through predicting future trends, the beverage titan was able to optimize inventory levels, minimizing losses from over-production of less popular products. It also led to greater supply chain efficiency, such as the orange juice project, which yielded significant cost savings.

The Lessons

Coca-Cola's success serves as an excellent case study illustrating the power of predictive analytics. It underscores that investing in predictive analytics can reap significant benefits for companies - from enhancing customer understanding to optimizing supply chain operations.

Perhaps, the biggest takeaway from this case study is the importance of an organization's willingness to embrace data and invest in building analytical capabilities. This necessitates both cultural and technological changes, but as Coca-Cola has demonstrated, the return on such investments can be significant.

VII. Developing a Predictive Analytics Framework

7.1 *Building a Strategic Predictive Analytics Framework*

A persuasive predictive analytics framework is more than just an amalgam of statistical tools and techniques. It requires a strategic, structured approach to leveraging data for decision-making. This subsection provides a comprehensive guide on developing a robust predictive analytics framework.

7.1.1 Defining Business Objectives

The establishment of any predictive analytics framework must always commence with the clear definition of business objectives. The criticality of this process cannot be overstressed for it sets the stage for the entire analytical operation. It subsequently facilitates the identification of key performance indicators (KPIs) that can be used to gauge progress towards meeting your business objectives.

7.1.2 Identifying Relevant Data Sources

Next, it is essential to determine what data sources are available and useful to meet your stated objectives. Data may stem from internal sources — such as databases, business software, and systems — or from external sources like social media, vendor databases, or third-party providers. It's also important to ascertain the need for both structured and unstructured data.

7.1.3 Data Collection and Integration

Data collection is a meticulous process whereby the identified data sources are harvested. Strategies for data collection extend from setup of APIs to scraping data from webpages. Following this, the accumulated data from different sources must be integrated, which often necessitates dealing with discrepancies in formats, granularity, or terminology.

7.1.4 Data Cleaning and Transformation

Data cleanliness impacts directly on the reliability of analytics. It involves scrutinizing and resolving issues of missing values, inconsistencies, or anomalies in the collected data. Subsequently, data transformation is carried out to convert the cleansed data into an appropriate format for modeling, which can entail activities like normalization, encoding categorical variables, or time-series conversion.

7.1.5 Exploratory Data Analysis

Before model building, it's crucial to explore and understand your data. Exploratory Data Analysis (EDA) involves visualizing data distributions, identifying correlations, and detecting outliers. It enlightens the data scientist on the underlying structures and patterns in the data and gives key insights that guide model creation.

7.1.6 Model Building and Evaluation

Model building is the heart of predictive analytics involving techniques like regression, decision trees, or neural networks, amongst others. The chosen method depends on the nature of data and the business problem. Following development, the model's performance must be evaluated using relevant metrics like accuracy, precision, recall, or ROC AUC, depending on the problem context.

Further, concepts like model validation and overfitting must be appreciated. Validation entails partitioning your data into a training set for model learning and a testing set for evaluation, ensuring that the model's performance is assessed independently from its learning. Overfitting, on the other hand, refers to when a model adapts too well to the training data that it performs poorly on unseen data.

7.1.7 Deployment and Monitoring

Once satisfactorily evaluated, the model is deployed into the business environment, integrated into operations or decision-making processes. However, deployment isn't the terminus of the framework. The model's performance needs to be monitored continually to ensure its predictive power remains reliable over time given the dynamic nature of data.

A predictive analytics framework, thus, requires a strategic, end-to-end approach that caters to the entire analytics lifecycle from objective determination to model deployment and monitoring. This description gives you the foundation to customize a framework fitting to your business circumstances, to harness the immense predictive potential inherent in your data.

VII.1. Understanding the Need for a Predictive Analytics Framework

Before diving into the technical particulars of developing a Predictive Analytics (PA) framework, it's important to understand what it is and why it is such a vital tool in today's business world. Predictive analytics is an advanced form of data analytics that uses data, statistical algorithms, machine learning techniques, and artificial intelligence to predict future outcomes based on past trends. By utilizing past performance to predict future behavior, predictive analytics provide businesses with actionable insights and the ability to make pro-active decisions.

A Predictive Analytics framework is a structured set of guidelines or protocols that help businesses in implementing predictive analytics. It offers a standardized process to follow, ensuring consistency and reliability in the analytics outcomes. A well-constructed PA framework ensures that you're not just generating predictions for the sake of it.

Instead, you're using these forecasts to drive meaningful change and optimize operational efficiency in your organization.

VII.2. Components of a Predictive Analytics Framework

Constructing a PA framework starts with understanding its essential components:

1. **Data Collection**: This is the foundation of the framework. It is the stage where data relevant to the study or prediction domain is gathered from various sources - both internal and external.
2. **Data Preprocessing**: Here, the collected data is cleaned and transformed into a format suitable for analysis. This step frequently involves handling missing values, removing outliers, feature scaling, and taking care of duplicated data.
3. **Data Analysis**: This step entails exploratory analytics to gain insights into the data and understand the underlying patterns and trends.
4. **Modeling**: Here, suitable predictive models are chosen based on the problem at hand and used to build the predictive analytics model.
5. **Validation**: This involves testing the constructed model against a set of data (test datasets) to validate its capability to effectively predict possible outcomes.
6. **Deployment**: Once validated, the model is deployed into the operational systems to start generating predictions.
7. **Monitoring & Maintenance**: This is an ongoing process that helps ensure the model stays relevant over time. The model's performance is regularly monitored and adjustments are made as required.

VII.3. Defining Business Objectives

The first step in developing a Predictive Analytics framework is to define clear business objectives. What do you want to achieve with your data? Is it improving customer retention, optimizing marketing strategies, or predicting future sales? Defining your objectives will guide you in determining the necessary data to be collected, the methods to use, and attaining meaningful results.

VII.4. Team Building

The next important step is assembling a team with the necessary skill set. This team should preferably comprise data scientists, machine learning experts, data engineers, business analysts, and domain experts. This diverse team ensures a comprehensive approach towards predictive analytics, bringing together different expertise and perspectives to the table.

VII.5. Data Management and Governance

Once the data is collected, it's important that you manage and govern it properly. This means maintaining data quality, ensuring data privacy and security, and complying with ever-evolving regulations.

Ultimately, developing a comprehensive Predictive Analytics framework may require significant resources and time, but the value it brings to your business in the long run outweighs the initial costs. It gives your business the ability to foresee potential challenges and opportunities, and make data-driven decisions crucial for growth and sustainability.

7.1 Understanding the Role of Data in Predictive Analytics Framework

Predictive analytics is a powerful tool built on the premise that the past can inform the future. By analyzing historical data, we can model and predict future outcomes, helping businesses make informed decisions based on expected scenarios. Critical to the success of this approach is a robust Predictive Analytics Framework, at the heart of which lies data. This chapter will delve into the importance of data in developing a framework and provide guidance on how to leverage it effectively.

7.1.1 Data Anatomy in Predictive Analytics

Data is the bedrock upon which predictive analysis is built. It's the language through which computers understand the world, and the raw material from which insights are extracted. At its essence, data in a predictive analytics context can be categorized into three main types based on its role in the predictive process:

- **Raw data**: This represents the unprocessed information collected from various sources. It can be anything from customer-behavior data on a website, sales data, marketing data, environmental data, to social media posts, among others.
- **Processed data**: This is the data that has been cleaned and manipulated for further analysis. Cleaning might involve removing or fixing errors, handling missing values, or resolving inconsistencies.
- **Output data**: This is the final product of the predictive analysis process. It includes the predictions and insights gleaned from the processed data that drive decision-making.

7.1.2 The Data Collection Process

Effective predictive analytics starts with data collection. The goal is to gather as much relevant and high-quality data as possible.

- One technique for collecting data is data mining, which involves actively extracting useful information from large datasets. To do this efficiently requires thorough planning and the right technological resources.
- Another approach involves big data technologies for handling data with high volume, high velocity, high variety, and high veracity (the four Vs of big data).
- Surveys and questionnaires can also form a reliable source of data, especially for collecting qualitative data about customer preferences and behaviors.

It's crucial that the data gathered is representative, accurate, and relevant to avoid creating models that are biased or hold no predictive power.

7.1.3 Data Preparation and Preprocessing

Once data is collected, the next step in the predictive analytics framework is preparing and preprocessing the data. This stage involves:

- **Data cleaning**: This involves identifying and correcting errors that may have occurred during the data collection process.
- **Data transformation**: This involves converting data into a suitable format for further analysis. The specific transformations used will depend on the requirements of the predictive model.

- **Feature engineering**: This step extracts valuable features from the data set to improve the predictive model's performance. These might include, for instance, creating a new variable that represents a customer's total spending over the past year.

7.1.4 Building Predictive Models

With clean, processed data in hand, the next step in developing a predictive analytics framework is to create predictive models using various techniques from statistics, data mining, and machine learning. Some commonly used predictive modeling techniques include:

- Regression analysis
- Decision trees
- Neural networks
- Ensemble methods
- Time series forecasting

Each method has its strengths and weaknesses, making it suitable for different types of data, problems, and objectives.

7.1.5 Model Validation and Evaluation

A critical final step in the predictive analytics framework is validating and evaluating the predictive models to ensure they're working as expected. This typically involves applying the model to a separate validation dataset and measuring its accuracy, preciseness, recall, and other metrics. These statistics provide critical feedback to guide adjustments to the model or the data preparation steps, leading to more reliable predictions.

In conclusion, data is the engine of the predictive analytics framework. Understanding its role and learning to manage it effectively can empower your business to harness predictive analytics' full potential. From data collection, through processing and modeling, all the way to validation, every step in the data life cycle feeds into and influences the ability to predict the future accurately.

Harnessing this power, companies can forecast trends, identify opportunities and risks, and build strategies that deliver results. In the uncertain realm of future prediction, a strong predictive analytics framework grounded in sound data practices is the closest thing we have to a crystal ball.

Section VII.1: Understanding and Defining the Business Problem in Predictive Analytics

Any effective predictive analytics framework starts with understanding and defining the business problem. The first crucial step before diving into data analysis and predictive modeling is to clearly identify the business question or problem that the analysis will address. This understanding informs every decision in the framework – from data collection to analysis, modeling, deployment, and monitoring.

Identify and Define the Business Problem

Understanding the business problem requires detailed knowledge about the business, industry, and marketplace. This knowledge will enable the team to ask relevant questions and define realistic goals. Ideally, the business problem should be a pressing issue that, if resolved, will have a significant impact on the business. The business problem should be defined explicitly, without any ambiguities.

Articulate the Objectives

Once the business problem is identified, the next step is to articulate the objectives. These objectives should be measurable, attainable, relevant, and time-bound (SMART). Articulating the objectives ensures that all team members, stakeholders, and decision-makers are on the same wavelength.

Determine the Scope of the Problem

Defining the scope of the business problem helps to provide concrete direction for the project. It involves clearly stating what is included and what is excluded from the analysis, which provides clarity to all team members and stakeholders.

Establish Hypotheses

Next, a hypothesis is developed based on the business problem. The predictive analytics team should generate hypotheses related to the problem and use these as starting points for the proposed solutions. Hypotheses formulation is a critical point in the predictive analytics framework as it helps in negating or proving certain assumptions related to the business problem.

Prioritize Possible Solutions

The final stage in understanding and defining the business problem is prioritizing possible solutions. The team should use their knowledge and experience to develop potential solutions, then assess and rank them based on their feasibility and potential impact.

Properly understanding and defining the business problem sets up the predictive analytics framework for success. It aids in the ideation of a feasible, high-impact solution that can be implemented to satisfy the business need identified at the beginning of the process. As the initial and essential step in predictive analytics, a thorough understanding of the business problem will yield better results, while a poorly defined or misunderstood problem can lead to wasted efforts and resources.

In the following sections, we will delve deeper into the subsequent stages of the predictive analytics framework, including data preparation, model selection, validation, deployment, and monitoring. The end goal is to harness the power of data to generate accurate forecasts and make informed future business decisions.

VII.I. Establishing a Solid Predictive Analytics Foundation

Before embarking on sophisticated predictive analytics projects, it's crucial to establish a robust predictive analytics framework. This framework will serve as the roadmap that guides you through the journey of transforming raw data into valuable decisions for your business.

a. Understanding the Business Context and Formulating Good Questions

Predictive analytics begins with a clear understanding of the issues at hand. Begin by determining what problems your business needs to solve or what opportunities it wants to capitalize on. This will lay the groundwork for your predictive analytics initiative and dictate what data you need, the type of analysis required, and the tools and resources necessary for the project.

b. Data Collection

Effective predictive analytics is driven by abundant data. However, gathering more data isn't necessarily better; you must collect the right data. This accomplishing this, you need to identify the data that relates to your business question, including internal data from your company's operational systems and external data from social media, websites, or third-party data providers.

c. Data Cleaning and Preprocessing

The collected data needs to be cleaned and preprocessed before analysis. This involves dealing with missing values, handling outliers, and standardizing the data. This methodology can prove to be a meticulous and time-consuming process, but it's crucial as it can significantly impact the quality of your predictive model.

d. Selecting Techniques and Building Models

The next step involves the selection of suitable predictive analytics techniques based on the nature of your problem and the data at hand. Some commonly used methods include regression analysis, time series forecasting, and machine learning techniques such as decision trees and neural networks. It's crucial to build several models and iterate to find the most accurate and useful for your given context.

e. Evaluating and Refining Models

Once you've built your predictive models, they need to be meticulously examined and refined. You should evaluate their performance against both the training and testing data sets. This involves various metrics, and the choice of these depends on your specific requirements and the nature of the problem at hand.

f. Implementation and Deployment

After your model has been refined and rechecked, it's time to implement it. This could mean integrating the model into a production environment where it can influence real-world decisions, or it might involve embedding the model into your operational systems to automate decision-making processes.

g. Monitoring and Maintenance

Deploying your model is not the end of the process. Predictive analytics is an ongoing process requiring consistent monitoring and maintenance. This includes regularly checking the model's performance, conducting systematic reviews, and making necessary adjustments to adapt to changes in underlying business dynamics and data patterns.

By following this framework, organizations can ensure they leverage predictive analytics effectively. But remember, predictive analytics is not just a one-off initiative. Instead, it should be woven into your everyday business processes, driving continuous learning, and decision-making.

VIII. Future Trends in Predictive Analytics

A. Predictive Analytics and AI Revolution

With a surge in computational power and the abundance of data available, artificial intelligence has greatly reshaped the way we understand and leverage predictive analytics. AI and machine learning methodologies have shown remarkable success when applied to predictive analytics projects. They have allowed for more accurate prediction and foretelling patterns that traditional statistical methods couldn't capture.

For years, organizations have been using predictive analytics to forecast future outcomes based on historical data. However, with the help of AI, businesses now can go even beyond that, to pick up patterns from vast and varied data sources like never before. This amalgamation of AI and predictive analytics is becoming the cornerstone in decision-making processes—ranging from customer segmentation in marketing to preventing fraud in the banking sector.

1. AI-driven Predictive Models

As we head into the future, we can expect AI-driven predictive models to become more complex and sophisticated. These models will not just predict future events, but can also predict multiple related events at the same time, providing a full future outlook. This will enable better decision-making as businesses can prepare for all possible future outcomes.

2. Real-time Predictive Analytics

We are ratcheting towards a real-time predictive analytics paradigm shift. Advances in AI and data analytics now enable real-time prediction of events. This means businesses can anticipate customer requirements, market changes or detect potential threats in real-time and take swift actions.

3. Explainable AI

In the future, we'll witness efforts towards improving the transparency of AI predictions. Unlike the traditional 'black box' nature of AI models, where the decision-making process is hard to understand, explainable AI strives to make the process transparent and easy to interpret. This will not only improve trust in AI systems but also enables the fine-tuning of models for more accurate predictions.

4. Autonomous Machines and Internet of Things (IoT)

With the proliferation of IoT devices and autonomous machines, predictive analytics will play a key role in forecasting equipment failures, optimizing supply chains, and improving operations. Predictive maintenance, powered by IoT sensors, can catching early signs of equipment failure, reducing downtime and repair costs.

5. Privacy and Security

As predictive analytics increasingly relies on AI, issues around privacy and security will undoubtedly become more salient. As AI models learn from more and more data, methodologies to ensure privacy protection and data anonymization in machine learning models will be crucial.

6. Predictive Analytics in the Cloud

The trend of moving predictive analytics into the cloud will persist, providing businesses with scalable, cost-effective, and remote solutions. Cloud-based predictive analytics software will also make it easier for organizations to incorporate and manage big data.

In conclusion, the future trends of predictive analytics are deeply intertwined with the growth of AI and machine learning technologies. As we move towards a data-driven future, harnessing the true power of predictive analytics will be pivotal in enabling smart, predictive decisions and building sustainable business models. It will transform the way we look at the world and revolutionize various sectors from healthcare to finance, retail to manufacturing, and beyond.

"Shifting Paradigms: Predictive Analytics and Artificial Intelligence"

As we peer into our crystal ball to take a glimpse of what the future holds for predictive analytics, one trend that stands out prominently is the amalgamation of predictive analytics and artificial intelligence (AI). It's an evolution that builds on harnessing the power of data for future insights and transcends toward creating systems that not only analyze but also learn from data.

In recent years, the inception and progress of AI have been revolutionary. AI holds the potential to significantly reshape various industries as it has brought about advancements in automation and analytics capable of processing vast data volumes.

AI and Predictive Models

Experts believe that the fusion of AI and predictive analytics will redefine the landscape of data analysis. AI's capacity for learning, perception, problem-solving, and decision-making coupled with predictive analytics' strength in forecasting future outcomes based on historical patterns sets the stage for powerful predictive models.

One way in which AI improves predictive analytics lies in its ability to process diverse data types. Traditionally, predictive models primarily worked with structured numerical data. But AI's ability to handle unstructured data, such as text, voice, image, and even video content, widens the scope of analytics and draws richer, deep-seated insights that might have been inaccessible otherwise.

Moreover, by enabling machines to understand and learn from data, AI can automatically refine predictive models over time. Thus, it mitigates the issue of model decay and ensures a better quality of future predictions.

Adopting AI in Businesses

Businesses, embracing this trend, have started exploiting AI-infused predictive analytics to automate processes, make data-informed strategic decisions, and provide personalized customer experiences.

- **Automating Business Processes**: Many businesses now leverage AI-based predictive models to automate routine tasks. From sales forecasting to risk assessment, AI handles it all, thereby freeing up human resources for more complex tasks and decision-making.
- **Strategic Decision Making**: With augmented data capabilities, businesses can predict trends, identify opportunities, and preemptively address potential

threats with more precision. This foresight provides a competitive edge in the ever-evolving business landscape and helps align strategies and operations more effectively.

- **Personalized Customer Experience**: One of the most notable applications of the AI-Predictive analytics synergy lies in personalization. Companies can predict customer behaviors, preferences, and potential churn, thereby offering a tailored customer journey that enhances engagement and fosters loyalty.

Challenges and The Way Forward

Despite the promising prospects, integrating AI in predictive analytics is not without challenges. The dependence on AI— and by extension, on data—raises significant concerns around data security and privacy. Additionally, businesses maneuvering through their initial stages of AI adoption often grapple with high upfront costs, operational alterations, lack of skilled resources, and regulatory discrepancies.

Despite these challenges, the merging of AI and predictive analytics holds immense potential. Technological advancements, coupled with an evolving understanding of data's value, make this a trend that cannot and should not be overlooked.

As we look ahead, it is imperative that businesses not only brace themselves for this shift but also actively seek ways to leverage the power of AI-integrated predictive analytics. As more businesses harness the compelling combination of predictive analysis and AI, innovation, efficiency, and accuracy will continue to thrive in the data-empowered landscape of the future.

1. The Impact of Artificial Intelligence on Predictive Analytics

With the continuous advancements in technology, Artificial Intelligence (AI) is increasingly becoming integral in predictive analytics. The potential for AI to learn from data sets enables it to make more accurate predictions based on the information it is fed. In essence, AI machines learn from historical data to predict future outcomes.

AI Models in Predictive Analytics

Several AI models are being used in predictive analytics, ranging from neural networks, decision trees, and genetic algorithms to fuzzy logic models and regression models. AI predictive models have the impressive ability to handle a vast amount of data from diverse sources and variables, making them effective in presenting more accurate predictions than traditional models.

Improved Predictive Accuracy

AI is fundamentally transforming predictive analytics by significantly enhancing predictive accuracy. Modern AI-powered algorithms can handle and interpret, with high accuracy, complex patterns within big data. In addition to dealing with structured data, AI also excels in handling unstructured data, enabling the generation of predictions from diverse data sources such as text, speech, and images.

Transformation of Industries with AI-assisted Predictive Analytics

AI-assisted predictive analytics is transforming numerous industries, with the healthcare, finance, and retail sectors more noticeably affected. In healthcare, predictive analytics is leveraged to anticipate disease outbreaks, diagnose diseases early, and enhance personalized treatments. In finance, AI is used to predict market trends, assess credit risk, and detect fraudulent activities. Retailers utilize AI to optimize inventory management, enhance customer experience, and anticipate consumer behavior and trends.

2. Arrival of Real-time Predictive Analytics

Another future trend in the world of predictive analytics is the advent of real-time predictive analytics. The need to make faster decisions in today's rapidly changing, data-driven world has given rise to this trend. By analyzing real-time data, relevant stakeholders can make instant, informed decisions.

Role of IoT in Real-time Predictive Analytics

The Internet of Things (IoT) is radically fast-tracking the implementation of real-time predictive analytics. With the proliferation of IoT devices, organizations can now access a continuous stream of real-time data, which can be analyzed instantaneously. This allows organizations to detect and address problems swiftly, thus mitigating risks and taking advantage of opportunities in real-time.

3. Automating Predictive Analytics

The automation of predictive analytics is yet another prospective trend that is set to revolutionize the analytics landscape. This involves using technology to perform tasks that would traditionally require human intervention.

Impact of Automation on Workforce

The automation of predictive analytics could lead to job loss. However, it is more likely to redefine job roles than eliminate them altogether. Instead of performing routine data analysis, data scientists can focus on interpreting and making decisions based on the data analysis results. Thus, automation is likely to lead to more efficient use of human resources.

These are just but a glimpse into the future of predictive analytics. As technology continues to evolve and become more sophisticated, it's exciting to think about the myriad of ways predictive analytics will transform how we make predictive decisions. This continual evolution further underscores the importance of harnessing the power of predictive analytics.

8.1 Predictive Analytics and Artificial Intelligence (AI)

The intersection of predictive analytics and artificial Intelligence (AI) is set to be one of the major trends in the future. AI has become a new standard of intelligent computing and is fast changing the landscape of predictive analytics. Predictive analytics relies heavily on algorithms and models that can quickly scan, analyze, and interpret vast datasets. An AI-based system has the ability to not only process this data at incredible speeds but also learn from it.

Machine learning, a subset of AI, is one of the key players in this shift. Algorithms learn from historical data, create patterns, and then make predictions about future data, enabling the automation of a significant number of processes. The increasing implementation of these tools is expected to hasten the development of predictive analytics.

8.2 Ubiquity of Predictive Analytics

Predictive analytics is expanding its horizons beyond industry & business applications. The future will see predictive analytics in everyday scenarios such as personal fitness, home security, agriculture, and even politics. Now, predictive tools are not just the forte of companies. A wide range of personal devices is enabling users to generate data and produce personalized predictions. This increasingly common presence is indicative of the growing importance and practicality of predictive analytics in varied walks of life.

8.3 The Cloud and Predictive Analytics

With the rise of cloud computing, predictive analytics has experienced considerable potential of growth. The cloud makes it easier to manage and analyze big data. Future trends point to predictive analytics moving towards cloud-based platforms. With increasing data availability in the cloud, organizations can leverage this flexibility and scalability to execute predictive analytics more efficiently, thus extracting valuable insights in real time.

8.4 Time-Sensitivity and Real Time Predictions

As we move further into the era of digital transformation, the significance of real-time data is increasing exponentially. Futuristic predictive analytics will not only be about accurate predictions but also about making these predictions in real time. Faster analytics and timely insights will become more critical in driving business decisions and strategic actions. The integration of streaming analytics in predictive models could prove to be a game-changer in this context.

8.5 Privacy and Security Concerns

With the advancement of predictive analytics, privacy and security concerns will also come under the spotlight. As a future trend, regulations around data privacy may become more stringent. Predictive analytics, which relies largely on data, will need to balance its goals with the necessary regulatory standards.

To conclude, the arenas of predictive analytics is dynamic and evolutionary. Innovations, such as AI and machine learning, are revolutionizing its capabilities and applications. Yet, it must be complemented by robust data governance policies to respect user-private data. Future trends indicate an exciting trajectory for this domain, with technology forever pushing the boundaries of what is possible.

Harnessing Machine Learning for Predictive Analytics

One of the most exciting future trends in predictive analytics is the integration of machine learning techniques into traditional statistical models. Machine learning, a subset of artificial intelligence, allows computers to learn from and make decisions based on data without being explicitly programmed.

Harnessing machine learning for predictive analytics means that the algorithms can continually learn from new data, and adapt accordingly. This presents a step change in predictive power, with modern machine learning models capable of outperforming traditional statistical techniques, especially on large and complex datasets.

Supervised and Unsupervised Learning

The crux of machine learning revolves around two types of learning – Supervised Learning and Unsupervised Learning.

In supervised learning, an algorithm is trained on a labelled dataset, meaning it has both the input parameters and the desired output. The algorithm learns the relationship between input and output during training and applies this knowledge to new, unseen data.

Unsupervised learning, on the other hand, works with datasets without labels. The goal in unsupervised learning is to find patterns and relationships in the data. Cluster analysis is a common unsupervised learning technique that groups data points based on similarity.

Deep Learning Revolution

A particular type of Machine Learning model called Deep Learning, has gained popularity over the past few years due to its capacity to learn from complex and vast datasets. Deep learning uses artificial neural networks with multiple layers (hence 'deep') to increase accuracy in tasks like object recognition, speech recognition, and now predictive analytics.

These models have proved incredibly successful at tasks where the solution involves mapping complex inputs to outputs and learning from examples. The advent of big data has given the deep learning revolution a significant boost because it thrives on utilizing large amounts of data to make accurate predictions or extract precise insights.

Real-Time Predictive Analytics

Another exciting trend in predictive analytics is real-time analysis. With today's computational power paired with machine learning models, we can perform predictive analytics in real-time, giving business leaders and decision-makers instant insights to inform their strategic initiatives.

The value of real-time predictive analytics extends not just to making better decisions faster, but also to adjusting actions or decisions in response to changing situations. It's a form of micro-strategizing that can inform granular level decisions "on the fly," and is particularly valuable for sectors where conditions can change rapidly, such as finance and retail.

Transparency and Ethical Concerns

As with all powerful tools, there are ethical questions related to the use of machine learning in predictive analytics. Issues of data privacy, transparency in how models make predictions, and the potential for algorithmic bias, are all significant concerns.

Recent strides have been made in developing 'explainable' machine learning models that can provide insights into how they arrived at a determination. However, many high-performance machine learning models are still considered as 'black boxes,' with little transparency into the internal decision-making process.

It is likely that transparency in machine learning will become a more significant issue in the future, as ethical and governance concerns grow, pushing for the development of interpretable and responsible AI.

In conclusion, harnessing machine learning techniques for predictive analytics presents an exciting and innovative future trend. The combination of advanced machine learning models, increased computational power, and vast data availability will undoubtedly drive breakthroughs in predictive analytics, opening up new opportunities and challenges.

IX. Challenges and Limitations of Predictive Analytics

Subsection - Understanding the Complexity and Ethical Implications of Predictive Analytics

Predictive analytics hold clear benefits for optimizing various processes and improving decision-making. Yet, while offering significant advantages, the efficient use of predictive analytics is not without its challenges. In fact, it presents significant complexity and ethical considerations which organizations need to understand and address adequately to ensure ethical and optimal use.

Data Quality and Management

Data quality significantly impacts the effectiveness of predictive analytics. The principle "garbage in, garbage out" rings true in predictive analytics. Invalid, incomplete, or biased data can lead to incorrect conclusions and flawed decision-making. Additionally, predictive analytics require substantial volumes of data, making data management another potential challenge. Issues in data storage, retrieval, and cleaning may arise, affecting the overall analytic process.

Model Accuracy

Predictive models rely on historic data and trends, with the assumption that future patterns will resemble past ones. However, novel events or unknown factors can distort this trend, resulting in inaccuracies. In these cases, predictive models may fail, leading to potentially harmful consequences. Hence, the challenge lies in improving model robustness and adaptability.

Skills Gap

The effective interpretation and implementation of predictive analytics require specialized skills. Often, organizations face a gap in expertise, which can hinder proper adoption. Training personnel, collaborating with experts, or leveraging automated tools are among the solutions to this limitation but come with their own challenges and costs.

Transparency and Trust

The complexity of predictive models can make it hard for non-experts to understand how they derive their predictions or recommendations. This lack of transparency can lead to mistrust and reduced adoption. Ensuring that models are interpretable and explainable can overcome this challenge, yet, it is often a trade-off with model accuracy and depth.

Regulatory Compliance

As predictive analytics relies on data, organizations must comply with various data protection and privacy laws, such as the General Data Protection Regulation (GDPR). These regulatory constraints can limit data usage and sharing, which can affect the performance of predictive models.

Ethical Implications

Predictive analytics can potentially trigger ethical controversies, particularly if results accidentally favor or discriminate against particular groups based on sensitive attributes like race, gender, or socio-economic status. Resulting biased decisions can reflect negatively on an organization's reputation and legal standing. Ethical data handling and use is a significant concern demanding a careful approach to predictive analytics' application.

Resistance to Change

Humans innately resist change; thus, transforming decision-making processes from manual to ones driven by data and technology can encounter resistance. Strategic change management that stresses the benefits and ensures stakeholder participation can help overcome this limitation.

Predictive analytics is a powerful tool, but it should be used mindfully and not seen as a magical solution. Recognizing these limitations and challenges will help organizations leverage predictive analytics in ethical, effective, and impactful ways.

In conclusion, understanding these challenges allows organizations to implement the right strategies to navigate these limitations and harness the true potential of predictive analytics, ensuring the future predictions they make are as accurate and valuable as possible. Employing predictive analytics responsibly allows organizations to enjoy the technology's benefits while ensuring they continue to operate within ethical boundaries, thereby maintaining public confidence and trust in their operations. It is evident that while predictive analytics can transform business operations, realizing its full potential requires careful consideration and navigation of the associated challenges and limitations.

Subsection: Understanding the Intricacies Involved in Predictive Analytics

While predictive analytics offer an impressive spectrum of advantages and opportunities to businesses in various industries, it is crucial that we acknowledge and understand its limitations as well. Several factors can hinder the effectiveness of predictive models, ranging from problems with data to challenges in implementation. Here is a detailed overview of some of the main challenges and limitations that predictive analytics presents:

1. **Data Quality Issues:** Predictive analytics largely depend on the quality of the data at hand. If the data is incomplete, inconsistent, outdated or inaccurate, the effectiveness of predictive analytics can be severely hindered. Data must be well-managed, regularly updated and thoroughly cleaned. Outliers must also be correctly treated as they can skew the results.

2. **Overfitting and Underfitting Models:** This can be a significant problem in predictive modeling. Overfitting occurs when the model is too complex and it starts to catch random noise instead of describing the underlying relationships. On the other hand, underfitting happens when the model is too simple to capture all the data relationships. Both overfitting and

underfitting can lead to inaccurate and unreliable predictions.

3. **Correlation Does Not Imply Causation:** Predictive analytics can identify patterns and relationships between different variables, but it cannot always establish the causal effect, i.e., whether one variable is the reason for the change in another. The failure to determine causal relationships can sometimes lead to misleading predictions.

4. **Time-Sensitive Data:** Predictive models developed using historical data might not hold accurate for the future if the data is strongly time-dependent. Changes in customer behavior, market trends, or environmental conditions can significantly impact the model's accuracy.

5. **Reliance on Domain Expertise:** Predictive analytics can suggest what might happen in the future, but deciding on the action to take based on that prediction often requires extensive domain knowledge. A predictive model can indicate the likelihood of customer churn, but the effective strategy to retain the customer needs domain expertise.

6. **Transparency and Trust:** Predictive models, especially those using complex algorithms, can be like 'black boxes' that generate predictions without providing a clear understanding of how they arrived at that prediction. This lack of transparency can hinder trust and hinder their wider acceptance.

7. **Ethical and Privacy Concerns:** Predictive analytics often require the use of sensitive personal data. However, it's essential to navigate through this responsibly. Not adhering to data privacy regulations and ethical considerations while dealing with such data can lead to serious repercussions.

8. **Long-Term Deployment and Maintenance:** As market patterns and customer behavior evolve,

predictive models need regular updating and maintenance to ensure continued accuracy and relevance. This can prove to be a challenging task requiring significant effort and resources.

While these challenges pose some difficulties, trying to achieve perfection in predictive analytics is often less valuable than simply making progress. The key is to be aware of these limitations and take steps to minimize their impacts. Despite the limitations listed, the advantages of predictive analytics far outweigh the difficulties, making it an essential tool in the modern business landscape. The key is not to solely rely on the technology but to leverage it in conjunction with human judgment and expertise.

IX.1 Understanding the Limits of Predictive Analytics

Although predictive analytics offers promising benefits, it's important to understand that the technology isn't foolproof and comes with its unique set of challenges and limitations. No predictive modeling technique can guarantee 100% accuracy – a degree of uncertainty is always prevalent.

1. Data Quality and Quantity

The accuracy of predictive analytics heavily relies on the quality and quantity of the data used. Using incomplete, incorrect, outdated, or biased data can lead to erroneous predictions. Moreover, predictive models require large volumes of data to function efficiently. If not enough data is available, the analytical model may yield inaccurate predictions.

2. Data Interpretation

Interpreting the results correctly is another challenge with predictive analytics. There are instances where models can predict an outcome that is inconsistent with the underlying reality. If the interpretation is incorrect, decisions based on these predictions can lead to undesirable outcomes. Models are only as good as the people interpreting them.

3. Overfitting and Underfitting

Predictive models, particularly those based on machine learning algorithms, can suffer from problems of overfitting and underfitting. Overfitting occurs when a model is overly complex and includes effects that are random rather than systematic, causing the model to fit too well to the specific data set and perform poorly with new data. On the other hand, underfitting happens when the model is too simple and fails to capture important trends in the data, resulting in poor predictions.

4. Timeliness of Predictions

The predictive power of models tends to degrade over time. This is because the underlying patterns and relationships in data can change. Models should be regularly updated and tested against recent data to ensure they remain valid.

5. Ethical and Privacy Concerns

Using predictive analytics can also raise ethical and privacy concerns. Models can sometimes reveal sensitive data or result in discriminatory practices, especially when the data includes personal identifiers. Therefore, it's crucial to respect privacy regulations and ethical standards when employing predictive analytics.

6. Cost and Time Intensive

The process of data collection, analysis, and model building for predictive analytics can be costly and time intensive. Furthermore, sufficient human intellect and time need to be invested in understanding and properly leveraging the results.

7. Dependence on Domain Knowledge

Finally, successful predictive analytics projects typically depend on significant subject matter expertise. While the process may have been automated, the insights that result from these models are not always obvious and can require deep domain expertise to realize and act on.

Identifying the implicit limitations and challenges of predictive analytics underlines the importance of continuous refinement and adjustment. Realizing that predictive models should not be used as primary decision-making tools but rather as supportive components, is a crucial element of effectively employing predictive analytics.

Obstacles to Incorporating Predictive Analytics

Although predictive analytics bears the potential to drastically transform businesses by offering valuable future insights, the implementation of this powerful tool unveils a unique set of challenges:

Data Quality:

One of the most critical aspects influencing the success or failure of a predictive model is the quality of data being used. Poor data quality can misguide predictions, leading to inaccurate conclusions and misguided strategies. It is estimated that poor-quality data costs the U.S economy over $3.1 trillion each year (source). Data cleansing, enrichment and validation can be time-consuming but are necessary steps in the data pre-processing phase.

Lack of Skilled Analysts:

Designing, implementing, and interpreting results from predictive analytics models often requires a blend of expertise in statistics, data science, and machine learning. However, there is a significant shortage of such skilled professionals, which can hinder the growth and application of predictive analytics. As per a report from McKinsey, the U.S could face a shortage of 140,000 to 190,000 professionals with deep analytical skills by 2028 (source)

Data Privacy and Security Concerns:

As predictive analytics leverages massive amounts of data, this also poses significant risks regarding data privacy and security. Organizations must ensure that they adhere to the necessary laws and regulations when dealing with sensitive data, such as GDPR in Europe and CCPA in California.

Implementation Costs:

Incorporating predictive analytic tools into existing operations can involve substantial investment concerning both financial resources and time. Costs associated with buying or developing predictive analytics software, training staff, and maintaining these systems can be significant.

Misinterpretation of Output:

Predictive models offer probabilities, not certainties. Businesses failing to understand this aspect correctly may place too much faith in a single output which could lead to incorrect actions. Therefore, understanding and interpreting the results correctly is important for organizations.

Ethical Considerations:

The deployment of predictive analytics can be seen as discriminatory if it uses data to unfairly target specific individuals or groups for actions. There are also concerns that predictive models might reinforce existing biases present in the data.

Limitations of Quantitative Analysis:

Predictive analytics mainly relies on quantitative analysis. However, some aspects such as human behavior, company culture, or broader social trends, are not easily quantifiable yet can significantly influence the accuracy of predictive models.

Dynamic Nature of Markets:

Markets are ever-evolving environments. A predictive model that works well today might not necessarily be suitable for future circumstances. Predictive analytics must constantly adapt and evolve to deliver valuable insights in such a dynamic scenario.

Despite these challenges, the rewards of incorporating predictive analytics into an organization's decision-making process can be enormous. With the right strategies and tools, businesses can overcome these challenges and harness the power of predictive analytics to drive growth. As the saying goes, "It's tough to make predictions, especially about the future" - but with predictive analytics, organizations are better equipped than ever to face this challenge.

Understanding the Limitations of Predictive Analytics Techniques

Despite the transformative power of predictive analytics, it's crucial to understand that predictive models are not infallible premonitions. They are intrinsically tied to the data they are based upon, the algorithms that are used to process that data, and the ability to iteratively improve upon the developed model. Several limitations inherent to predictive analytics supply valuable lessons about how this technology can be effectively implemented and consciously understood.

Data Quality and Completeness

The adage "garbage in, garbage out" holds true in the world of predictive analytics. Models are only as good as the data feeding into them. Predictive analytics require clean, high-quality and properly formatted data in order to generate accurate and trustworthy predictions. Data which is inaccurate, incomplete, or biased can lead to models that yield misleading or negatively skewed predictions.

Similarly, even well-collected data has its limitations as it only represents past and present factors. If unexpected or unprecedented events (such as a global pandemic or economic meltdown) occur, the model may significantly underperform since it has no prior data to base such predictions on.

Model Complexity and Overfitting

The complexity of the model can also serve as a limitation. Complex models might perform exceptionally well on training data but fail miserably on new data because they have overfit the training data. Overfitting happens when a model learns the detail and noise in the training data to the extent that it negatively impacts the performance of the model on new data. This means that the noise or random fluctuations in the training data is picked up and learned as concepts by the model, making it less accurate when predicting outcomes for new data instances.

Uncertainty and False Positives

Uncertainty is another limitation of predictive analytics. While predictions are generated, it may be difficult to pinpoint the precise probability of occurrence due to the ever-changing nature of external factors. Additionally, a model may generate predictions with a certain degree of error, also known as false positives or false negatives. These false predictions can lead to resource-wasting or ill-informed decisions if not correctly identified and managed.

Ethical and Privacy Concerns

As predictive models often require extensive data, there may be issues related to privacy and data protection. Moreover, predictive analytics can inadvertently lead to ethical dilemmas. For instance, biased data can lead to biased predictions, furthering discriminatory outcomes even if unconsciously. Recognizing and mitigating these potential biases is crucial for responsible use of predictive analytics.

Evolving Technology

As technology continues to evolve, so too does the landscape of predictive analytics. New methods and approaches continually emerge while older ones mature or fade into obsolescence. This can make it challenging to select the appropriate method and can even necessitate switching strategies midway during the model designing or deployment stage.

Measure your predictive analytics effectiveness not just in terms of its accuracy, but also by appreciating its limitations and by constantly questioning the quality of your input data, the suitability of your chosen model, the clarity of your defined outcomes, and the impact of unforeseen external variables. Only then can you fully harness the true power of predictive analytics in forecasting and shaping future events.

X. Turning Predictive Analytics into Actionable Insights

X.I. Understanding the Basics of Actionable Insights

To fully comprehend how predictive analytics can be turned into actionable insights, it is crucial to first understand what actionable insights encompass. An actionable insight is information that a business can rely on to make strategic decisions. It offers managers tangible information which, when acted upon, makes it feasible to enhance business operations, customer experience, and ultimately, the bottom line. These insights are derived from analyzed data that reveal trends, patterns, and associations concerning the behavior of consumers and the performance of the business.

In the context of predictive analytics, these insights could come in the form of predictions about future trends, customer behavior, market developments, and other operational metrics essential to business success. Some examples are forecasting customer churn, predicting future sales, and estimating the effects of specific business decisions.

X.II. The Process of Creating Actionable Insights

Predictive analytics, a component of data analytics, primarily focuses on the utilization of data, statistical algorithm and AI techniques, to identify the likelihood of future outcomes based on historical data. Generating actionable insights through predictive analytics can be accomplished through a defined process that involves the following stages:

1. **Data collection:** The process commences with gathering of data from diverse sources such as business systems, customer feedback platforms, social media, customer interaction channels, public databases, etc. The richness and variety of data collected at this phase play a crucial role in the quality of insights that will be generated.
2. **Data cleaning and preparation:** This step involves the removal of errors, duplicate information, irrelevant data, and any other discrepancies that could compromise the reliability of the actionable insights produced.
3. **Analysis:** This is the stage where predictive models are built and applied, often using advanced algorithms and machine learning techniques. The primary purpose of this phase is to identify patterns and relationships among variables in the data that can be analyzed to predict future outcomes.
4. **Insight generation:** This is where the results of the analysis are, interpreted and translated into insights

or recommendations that are directly applicable to business operations or strategies.

5. **Implementation:** The final phase involves using the insights to inform decision making and action planning. This can involve a diverse range of actions, depending on the specific insights derived and the nature of the business.

X.III. The Value of Actionable Insights in Predictive Analytics

Transforming predictive analytics into actionable insights is of paramount importance because it's this transformation that adds value to an organization. Predictive analytics alone are great for anticipating what might happen in the future. However, without converting these predictions into actionable strategies, the information is essentially of little use.

For instance, if predictive analytics reveal that a business is at risk of losing a considerable portion of their customers in the next quarter, the actionable insight may guide the business to invest in customer retention programs.

Furthermore, actionable insights offer a tangible point of reference for strategic planning. Instead of vague notions or assumptions about business performance and market conditions, businesses can leverage these insights to make data-driven decisions that steer the company closer to its goals.

In conclusion, while predictive analytics act as the eyes that help businesses see the probable future, actionable insights are the feet that help these businesses move strategically towards future success.

X.Y Understanding Actionable Insights and Their Importance

Before we delve into how to turn predictive analytics into actionable insights, it is important to understand what actionable insights are and why they are crucial in the technologically driven business landscape.

The term 'actionable insight' refers to valuable information unearthed from your data that can be acted upon to improve business strategies and operations. In the realm of data analytics, it translates to the knowledge gained from statistical trends and patterns and converted into a strategy or action. An actionable insight is not just about understanding the hidden information in the data but also about turning that understanding into appropriate actions, effectively supporting decision-making processes.

The importance of these insights cannot be overstressed. In today's competitive business environment, organizations that can quickly leverage actionable insights to adapt to changes have a strategic advantage. Using these insights, businesses can build more accurate forecasts, optimize processes, improve customer satisfaction, increase revenue, reduce costs, and make more informed strategic decisions. Further, actionable insights provide a solid foundation for aligning business strategies and processes with customer needs and market trends, ultimately leading to better competitive positioning and long-term success.

X.Y.1 Translating Predictive Analytics into Actionable Insights

Now, let's look at how predictive analytics can be translated into actionable insights.

1. **Quality Data Collection**: The first step in generating actionable insights from predictive analytics involves gathering quality data. Ensure that data collection processes are robust enough to capture accurate and representative data from different facets of your business. Additionally, stay aware of potential biases in your data to maintain objectivity in the predictions.

2. **Analyze and Interpret the Data**: Next, apply data mining, statistical algorithms, and machine learning techniques to analyze the collected data and to identify patterns and trends. Here, different predictive models may be used to frame the probable future outcomes. The interpretations made here act as the bedrock of your actionable insights.

3. **Synthesize the Results into a Strategy**: Once the predictive patterns are discerned, combine the results into a feasible strategy. This includes making decisions about which predictions are most important for your business, translating quantitative outcomes into qualitative insights, and then into actions to be implemented.

4. **Implementing the insights**: After understanding what the results signify and developing a responsive strategy, the next step is to put the plan into action. Timely and effective implementation of the strategy is critical to making the most of your insights.

5. **Monitoring and Adapting**: Finally, as the actions drawn from predictive analytics are implemented, continual monitoring of the outcomes is crucial. This allows businesses to adapt and tweak their strategies based on real-time feedback and to evolve with the dynamic business environment.

X.Y.2 Challenges in Harnessing Actionable Insights

While predictive analytics has the potential to unlock a wealth of actionable insights, there are challenges to overcome. These include dealing with big data's volume, velocity, and variety, ensuring data quality and security, and translating complex predictive results into actions. A lack of skilled data professionals and the dynamic nature of data trends and algorithms can also pose challenges.

Despite these challenges, harnessing actionable insights from predictive analytics is an investment that can yield enormous returns. By combining technological advances, statistical expertise, and strategic foresight, businesses can turn mountains of data into gold mines of actionable insights. Therefore, a continuous commitment to refining data collection, analysis, and action plans is imperative for businesses to successfully harness the power of predictive analytics.

X.1 Operationalizing Predictive Analytics: How to Implement Actionable Insights

Understanding the patterns and trends in your data is one necessary step, but the real power of predictive analytics lies in its ability to spur meaningful actions. Given this, it's crucial to operationalize your predictive analytics process effectively.

X.1.1 Define Actionable Metrics

Begin by defining the metrics that are most relevant to your specific business goals. These might include customer churn rate, marketing campaign conversion rate, monthly active users, average revenue per user, etc. Once you have chosen the key metrics, model your predictive analytics process around them.

X.1.2 Building Robust Predictive Models

Your actionable metrics should guide the development of your predictive models. Consider, for instance, if your goal is to reduce customer churn. Your predictive model might utilize customer behavior data and engagement metrics to predict those at risk of churning. Once the model is developed, constantly iterate and refine it to enhance its predictive ability.

X.1.3 Customize Action Plans

Based on the predictions of your models, devise suitable action plans. These should be concrete, attainable tasks that can be carried out by your team. Sticking to our churn example, an action plan might be to reach out to at-risk customers with personalized offers or conduct a feedback survey to uncover the causes of dissatisfaction.

X.1.4 Automated Response Systems

Incorporate the use of automated response systems as much as possible in your action plans. For instance, an email marketing system could automatically segmentation the customers based on their risk level and send them targeted emails. This not only makes your process efficient but also ensures timely responses.

X.1.5 Foster Communication

Deploy predictive analytics insights across all relevant internal teams. This may involve the design of intuitive dashboards that convey the insights clearly and compellingly, and training team members on how to interpret the data and implement the decisions.

X.1.6 Measure Outcomes

Last but not least, it's essential to review and measure the outcomes of the actions taken. As actions get executed, results should be continuously monitored to assess the effectiveness and recalibrate the models if necessary. This forms a cycle of iterative improvement that continuously refines your predictive analytics process and its impact on your real-world business operations.

In summary, converting predictive analytics into actionable insights is not an one-off task. It involves a disciplined approach to iteratively building predictive models, implementing actions, monitoring results, and refining the methods. The rewards, however, are plentiful, as businesses that succeed in this task gain a tangible, data-driven guide to their future operations.

X.1 Utilization of Predictive Analysis Outputs

The primary purpose of predictive analytics is to extract valuable insights from data and utilize this information to predict future patterns, trends, and behaviors. However, the raw outputs of predictive analytics alone aren't necessarily "actionable". To fully realize the power of these predictive models, it is essential to convert these raw outputs into actionable insights that can be leveraged in decision-making processes.

X.1.1 Interpreting Predictive Analysis Outputs

The first step in turning predictive analytics into actionable insights is proper interpretation of the output data. This process requires a deep understanding of the predictive model, the data that was used, and the output itself. Analysts must clarify whether the model was a success in identifying patterns and making accurate predictions. Simple metrics such as accuracy, precision, recall, and F1-score can provide a quick insight into the model's performance. However, these metrics should be interpreted with caution, considering potential overfitting or underfitting of the model.

A comprehensive understanding of the predictive models allows businesses to identify potential flaws inherent to these models, thereby supporting the creation of better strategies or making necessary adjustments for future predictions.

X.1.2 Making Predictions Actionable

Once the predictions have been accurately interpreted, they can be converted into actionable insights. Depending on the context, different approaches might be applicable. For instance, in a sales scenario, predictions can be used to identify potential high-revenue customers, trigger targeted marketing efforts, or plan strategic pricing strategies. In a production setting, maintenance schedules or parts replacements could be adjusted based on predictive failure rates.

X.1.3 Connecting Insights with Decision Making

The ultimate goal of actionable insights is to feed into decision-making processes. By integrating predictive analytics into business operations, companies can take data-driven decisions, allowing them to gain a competitive edge. However, the integration of predictive analytics needs to be thoughtfully approached. It's crucial to ensure that businesses do not over-rely on data-driven decisions without incorporating human elements like creativity and intuition.

Additionally, the effectiveness of integrating predictive analytics into decision making largely depends on the organization's culture towards data-driven decision making and its openness to adopt change. Therefore, organizations need to ensure that they are fostering a data-centric culture while building robust change-management mechanisms.

X.1.4 Visualizing Predictive Analytics

Transforming raw data into a visual format is another key element in making predictive analytics entirely actionable. Data visualization tools such as charts, infographics, heat maps, etc., can make complex data more understandable, insightful, and usable. For example, plotting the projected sales of a product over the next quarter can visually demonstrate patterns and trends, making the numbers more tangible and meaningful.

In conclusion, turning predictive analytics into actionable insights is a process that requires proper interpretation of the output data, making the predictions actionable, integrating them into decision-making processes, and representing them visually. These insights don't just indicate what may occur in the future; they also provide valuable instructions about what steps should be taken now to leverage predicted outcomes or mitigate potential risks.

"Turning Predictive Analytics into Actionable Insights"

A. Understanding the Power of Predictive Analytics

Predictive analytics is an advanced form of analytics that uses historical data, statistical algorithms, and machine learning techniques to predict future outcomes. This tool is used by companies in various sectors, like healthcare, marketing, retail, finance, and more, to make well-informed decisions and strategies about the future.

In essence, predictive analytics harnesses the power of data to give insights into what is most likely to happen in the future. It leverages a variety of statistical, modeling, data mining, and machine learning techniques to study the past performance in order to predict the future outcomes.

Predictive models capture the relationships among various data elements and look for patterns or trends unraveled within these relationships to predict future risks and opportunities. By decoding these underlying patterns and potential trends, organizations can understand how different variables influence their business's trajectory, thereby making more informed, data-driven decisions.

B. Transforming Predictive Intelligence into Actionable Insights

While predictive analysis provides us with a probable future outcome, it's important to remember that knowing the future alone isn't enough; what counts is how we use this knowledge to our advantage. In other words, predictive analytics must be converted into actionable insights to drive effective decision-making.

Here's how you can do that:

- **Decision-Making:** Use predictive analytics to make informed decisions about the allocation of resources, risk management, and strategic planning. For example, retailers can use data about customers' previous purchases and preferences to predict what products will sell best in the future and stock inventory accordingly.
- **Strategic Planning:** Predictive analytics can help companies plan their next steps by providing insights into the future. For example, companies can use the insights to plan their marketing strategies by understanding what type of content engages their audience the most, or in which region their products are likely to sell more.
- **Risk Management:** Predictive analytics also plays a crucial role in identifying potential risks and taking preventative measures. For instance, financial institutions can leverage predictive analytics to assess a potential borrower's credit risk. Similarly, companies can anticipate equipment failures or interruptions in the production chain by analyzing operational data.
- **Personalization:** By understanding past customer behavior, predictive analytics allows businesses to offer personalized customer experiences. This aspect assists in developing stronger customer relationships and encourages loyalty, which ultimately enhances your company's profitability.

C. Pitfalls to Avoid When Generating Actionable Insights

Now while predictive analytics can help businesses analyze complex data sets and predict future outcomes, it's essential to avoid certain pitfalls when generating actionable insights:

- **Data Quality:** The accuracy of your predictions largely depends on the quality of the data you analyze. Using inadequate, outdated, or irrelevant data can vastly skew your outcomes and lead to incorrect conclusions. Hence, ensure that your data is complete, relevant, and up to date.
- **Bandwagon Effect:** Don't blindly follow the trend; not every analytic prediction is suitable for all businesses. What works for one company may not necessarily work for another. Therefore, it's essential to determine the right predictive analysis tool that suits your company's specific needs and objectives.
- **Failure to Act:** Merely identifying the possibilities does not bring any value unless action is taken. The key here is to effectively translate those insights into actions that align with your business objectives.
- **Implementing in Silos:** Predictive analytics shouldn't be used in isolation to a single business function. For maximum impact, integrate predictive analytics across various departments to leverage the full potential of your data.

Remember, predictive analytics isn't a crystal ball that magically predicts the future. Still, when coupled with strategic actionable insights, it could be a game-changer in your decision-making process, driving growth and long-term success for your business.

Copyrights and Content Disclaimers:

DELAYS IN THE CONTENT OR TRANSMISSION OF THE DATA ON OUR book, OR THAT THE BOOK WILL ALWAYS BE AVAILABLE.

In addition to the above, it is important to note that language models like ChatGPT are based on deep learning techniques and have been trained on vast amounts of text data to generate human-like text. This text data includes a variety of sources such as books, articles, websites, and much more. This training process allows the model to learn patterns and relationships within the text and generate outputs that are coherent and contextually appropriate.

Language models like ChatGPT can be used in a variety of applications, including but not limited to, customer service, content creation, and language translation. In customer service, for example, language models can be used to answer customer inquiries quickly and accurately, freeing up human agents to handle more complex tasks. In content creation, language models can be used to generate articles, summaries, and captions, saving time and effort for content creators. In language translation, language models can assist in translating text from one language to another with high accuracy, helping to break down language barriers.

It's important to keep in mind, however, that while language models have made great strides in generating human-like text, they are not perfect. There are still limitations to the model's understanding of the context and meaning of the text, and it may generate outputs that are incorrect or offensive. As such, it's important to use language models with caution and always verify the accuracy of the outputs generated by the model.

Financial Disclaimer

This book is dedicated to helping you understand the world of online investing, removing any fears you may have about getting started and helping you choose good investments. Our goal is to help you take control of your financial well-being by delivering a solid financial education and responsible investing strategies. However, the information contained on this book and in our services is for general information and educational purposes only. It is not intended as a substitute for legal, commercial and/or financial advice from a licensed professional. The business of online investing is a complicated matter that requires serious financial due diligence for each investment in order to be successful. You are strongly advised to seek the services of qualified, competent professionals prior to engaging in any investment that may impact you finances. This information is provided by this book, including how it was made, collectively referred to as the "Services."

Be Careful With Your Money. Only use strategies that you both understand the potential risks of and are comfortable taking. It is your responsibility to invest wisely and to safeguard your personal and financial information.

We believe we have a great community of investors looking to achieve and help each other achieve financial success through investing. Accordingly we encourage people to comment on our blog and possibly in the future our forum. Many people will contribute in this matter, however, there will be times when people provide misleading, deceptive or incorrect information, unintentionally or otherwise.

You should NEVER rely upon any information or opinions you read on this book, or any book that we may link to. The information you read here and in our services should be used as a launching point for your OWN RESEARCH into various companies and investing strategies so that you can make an informed decision about where and how to invest your money.

WE DO NOT GUARANTEE THE VERACITY, RELIABILITY OR COMPLETENESS OF ANY INFORMATION PROVIDED IN THE COMMENTS, FORUM OR OTHER PUBLIC AREAS OF THE book OR IN ANY HYPERLINK APPEARING ON OUR book.

Our Services are provided to help you to understand how to make good investment and personal financial decisions for yourself. You are solely responsible for the investment decisions you make. We will not be responsible for any errors or omissions on the book including in articles or postings, for hyperlinks embedded in messages, or for any results obtained from the use of such information. Nor, will we be liable for any loss or damage, including consequential damages, if any, caused by a reader's reliance on any information obtained through the use of our Services. Please do not use our book If you do not accept self-responsibility for your actions.

The U.S. Securities and Exchange Commission, (SEC), has published additional information on Cyberfraud to help you recognize and combat it effectively. You can also get additional help about online investment schemes and how to avoid them at the following books:http://www.sec.gov and http://www.finra.org, and http://www.nasaa.org these are each organizations set-up to help protect online investors.

If you choose ignore our advice and do not do independent research of the various industries, companies, and stocks, you intend to invest in and rely solely on information, "tips," or opinions found on our book – you agree that you have made a conscious, personal decision of your own free will and will not try to hold us responsible for the results thereof under any circumstance. The Services offered herein is not for the purpose of acting as your personal investment advisor. We do not know all the relevant facts about you and/or your individual needs, and we do not represent or claim that any of our Services are suitable for your needs. You should seek a registered investment advisor if you are looking for personalized advice.

Links to Other Sites. You will also be able to link to other books from time to time, through our Site. We do not have any control over the content or actions of the books we link to and will not be liable for anything that occurs in connection with the use of such books. The inclusion of any links, unless otherwise expressly stated, should not be seen as an endorsement or recommendation of that book or the views expressed therein. You, and only you, are responsible for doing your own due diligence on any book prior to doing any business with them.

Liability Disclaimers and Limitations: Under no circumstances, including but not limited to negligence, will we, nor our partners if any, or any of our affiliates, be held responsible or liable, directly or indirectly, for any loss or damage, whatsoever arising out of, or in connection with, the use of our Services, including without limitation, direct, indirect, consequential, unexpected, special, exemplary or other damages that may result, including but not limited to economic loss, injury, illness or death or any other type of loss or damage, or unexpected or adverse reactions to suggestions contained herein or otherwise caused or alleged to have been caused to you in connection with your use of any advice, goods or services you receive on the Site, regardless of the source, or any other book that you may have visited via links from our book, even if advised of the possibility of such damages.

Applicable law may not allow the limitation or exclusion of liability or incidental or consequential damages (including but not limited to lost data), so the above limitation or exclusion may not apply to you. However, in no event shall the total liability to you by us for all damages, losses, and causes of action (whether in contract, tort, or otherwise) exceed the amount paid by you to us, if any, for the use of our Services, if any. And by using our Site you expressly agree not to try to hold us liable for any consequences that result based on your use of our Services or the information provided therein, at any time, or for any reason, regardless of the circumstances.

Specific Results Disclaimer. We are dedicated to helping you take control of your financial well-being through education and investment. We provide strategies, opinions, resources and other Services that are specifically designed to cut through the noise and hype to help you make better personal finance and investment decisions. However, there is no way to guarantee any strategy or technique to be 100% effective, as results will vary by individual, and the effort and commitment they make toward achieving their goal. And, unfortunately we don't know you. Therefore, in using and/or purchasing our services you expressly agree that the results you receive from the use of those Services are solely up to you. In addition, you also expressly agree that all risks of use and any consequences of such use shall be borne exclusively by you. And that you will not to try to hold us liable at any time, or for any reason, regardless of the circumstances.

As stipulated by law, we can not and do not make any guarantees about your ability to achieve any particular results by using any Service purchased through our book. Nothing on this page, our book, or any of our services is a promise or guarantee of results, including that you will make any particular amount of money or, any money at all, you also understand, that all investments come with some risk and you may actually lose money while investing. Accordingly, any results stated on our book, in the form of testimonials, case studies or otherwise are illustrative of concepts only and should not be considered average results, or promises for actual or future performance.

tolerance, and the ability to consistently apply the strategies and techniques discussed.